THE SLOPE OF THE WIND

THE SLOPE
OF THE WIND

Adrian Seligman

Seafarer Books

© 1994 Seafarer Books

First published by Seafarer Books
10 Malden Road, London NW5 3HR

ISBN 0 85036 443 4

Distributed in the United States by
Sheridan House, Inc.

Produced for Seafarer Books by
Chase Production Services, Chipping Norton OX7 5QR
Printed in Finland by WSOY

Sea People

... They are humble at heart, like the ships themselves. And a sailing ship at sea is one of God's most patient, yet most steadfast and courageous creatures. So those who live with her, who watch her day by day, running bravely, lying becalmed for weeks or yielding with grace to the slope of the wind, such people learn from her in time ...

Contents

Introduction

by Eric Newby

This book is an epic of the sea and the men who sailed on it in the big steel barques and barquentines owned by Gustav Erikson of Mariehamn in the Baltic.

In it Adrian Seligman describes with great vividness, accuracy and humour his early years as a sailor of the sail in two of these ships, *Killoran* and *Olivebank*, making altogether three circumnavigations of the world, a total of some 90,000 sea miles, while engaging in the Australian grain trade, each time returning to Europe by way of Cape Horn. And finally a stormy passage from the Baltic to London in one of the Company's timber barques.

His book begins in the summer of 1930, when he leaves Cambridge having failed his exams – something which causes his father to choke over his strawberries and cream. At the same time he receives a 'charmingly courteous threatening letter' from his bank manager and his girl-friend leaves him.

What more reasons one may well ask, would he have needed to make him decide to go to sea? Many a young man before him decided that a voyage was all that he really needed to resolve these and similar problems. (I myself took the decision when someone in the rush hour on the London Underground took my handkerchief out of the breast pocket of my jacket, blew his nose on it and put it back under the impression that it was his own.) Many answered the call to the sea and made a round voyage in an Erikson ship, comparatively few repeated the experience.

Adrian was different. He really wanted to be a sailor. He started his career in an eighty-foot diesel-engined coaster as a cook, joining her in a rat-infested backwater in the Thames Marshes, and subsequently almost put her on the Goodwin Sands while acting as helmsman. Then he went on to make his first deep sea voyage to Australia and back. It is all here, the life of a sailor: the fear of going aloft for the first time; the perils that attend an engineless sailing ship in soundings; the landfalls in Australia, Patagonia and Europe, unforgettable to sailors after weeks and months at sea; the wet, the cold, the tussels with board hard canvas aloft in the rigging, often in pitch darkness; the food, the senseless fights in the watch below; the agonising splits in one's fingers, never forgotten. And there are idyllic, and not so idyllic, interludes of fishing in the Baltic between voyages, and falling in love. They made a sailor of him. There is no doubt about that.

Prologue

Canvas Castles

People are apt to be on the defensive about sailing ships, and one can't altogether blame them. There's been too much bragging about 'the good old days' by those who knew them. Yet life in a sailing ship need be neither tough nor dangerous, and usually isn't. But what *is* true is that a sailing ship's crew are more personally involved in the ship's own struggle, against calms and gales and fitful weather, than steamer men.

They're closer to the sea. It comes aboard sometimes and knocks them down. They haul on ropes. They climb aloft to set or stow the sails. And when they are steering, they can *feel* the ship answering, or sometimes fighting, against her helm. They feel her lift and lunge and lean to the wind. They become part of her in a way no steamer man could ever become part of his ship. And in so doing, they grow closer to each other. Fellow-feeling, that's what the sea breeds. And sailing ships breed it best of all.

A voyage home from Australia used to take many months, with long spells of calm in the tropics or in the horse latitudes of the North and South Atlantic. It was then, in our canvas castles, on a flat and limitless sea, that we began to lose all sense of nationality and become, as it were, a race apart.

During the war, before we formed the Levant Schooner Flotilla, I was in a sort of Q-ship operating in enemy waters. And one day, by bad luck, we took a prisoner. He was an Italian soldier, called Mario. We fished him out of the water and then realised that we hadn't really room for him on board, nor any means of sending him down to base either. We couldn't quite bring ourselves to chuck him back. So we made him our cook instead.

Now you may think that was dangerous. He might have tried to poison us. But, after all, why should he – in a ship at sea, where we all relied so much upon each other? What would he have got out of it?

We grew very fond of Mario, and he soon got a nickname – 'Mix-up' – because of his cheery way of announcing meals: 'Mario mix up dinner' or just 'Mix up tea. Come.' We grew even fonder of his cooking, which really was excellent. So we were pretty down-hearted when one day we were forced to take shelter in a neutral harbour. Because all Mario had to do then was shout to one of the neutral sentries that he was a prisoner, and we'd have been forced to give him up.

But he didn't. And none of us really knew why. Unless one can accept his own reason, which was a simple one. 'If Mario leaving ship' he said, with a rather touching air of self-importance, 'who then make right mix up?'

Part I
Extraordinary Seaman

1.

Of Docks and Locks
and a Bar of Sunlight

The glowing summer of 1930 belonged to those magical days between the wars when everything seemed golden and everlasting. The pear trees blossomed early, the swifts came soon after and by July we were having strawberries and cream with every meal, including breakfast.

It was at one of those breakfasts that I realised, all at once, that for me the golden days were over. I wasn't really sorry. There had been a series of shocks: I'd failed my Mays at Cambridge; my father was so angry that he forgot to put sugar on his strawberries, which made him angrier still; my bank manager had sent me a charmingly courteous threatening letter, and by the same post Sheila had written to say that she was going to get married. I decided on the spot to go. There was really nothing else to do but start again – from a different angle, with a different objective and in a totally different environment. I packed a bag, tore up my bank manager's letter, put Sheila's in my pocket and caught a train to Aldgate East.

In those days it was possible to walk aboard any ship you liked the look of and get a job. It may be still in some ports, for all I know; but in those days it was a normal part of the average tramping seaman's life. He made a voyage of a year or more, then paid off with two or three hundred pounds in his pocket which he proceeded to spend on riotous living of one kind or another; or on absurd luxuries like a Daimler hire car for a week, or a box at the opera and a suit of dress clothes to go with it. And when all his money was gone, he just put on his dungarees and a cloth cap and wandered down to the docks to find himself a ship.

With me it wasn't quite the same, of course. I'd had what is sometimes known as a sheltered childhood; that is, I'd been sent off at the age of thirteen to join a few hundred other young savages at boarding school, who battered and hammered me about until I was big enough to do a bit of hammering myself. This was followed by two comparatively civilised years at University – hopelessly pampered and pleased with oneself, of course, but without any real plans for the future.

And now the Red Ensign Club, Dock Street, E1, where you paid ninepence a night (nine old pence that is) and no questions asked. If they had been, I couldn't have answered them. I had only one vague idea in my mind – to find out, if I could, what the world was really made of – but no very clear conception of how to set about it.

I made a few friends and with them joined the queues of unemployed at dock gates and shipping offices. I found myself part of a floating population which drifted like blown leaves from vessel to vessel and dock to dock – losing a few here and there, where jobs were going, picking up others, and congregating at pubs and sailors' homes in the evening to exchange the day's news of ships and mates and second mates and second stewards, of trades and cargoes and distant ports, of jobs in the offing and jobs refused.

It was a world of breath-taking romance to a boy of twenty just down from Cambridge – a world of feverish activity, stretching eastwards from London Bridge in mile after mile of docks and wharves, canals and locks and bridges, and the blind blank warehouse walls of Wapping and Stepney; with masts and funnels, cranes nodding over the bellies of great ships, shouting stevedores, seamen of every race and colour. And at night, blinding clusters of lights, the smell of steam, of spice, of timber from the jungle or the Arctic Circle; bananas, nuts, esparto grass and wine ... but no jobs, at least not yet.

August was blazing hot. I can still taste and smell the dust swirling round the corners of sheds or rising in clouds from open ships' hatches. I joined the stewards moving from dock to dock and was soon accepted as one of them. In fact, to my astonishment, after a couple of weeks I found myself, so to speak, the oldest inhabitant – the one who'd been longest looking for a berth and therefore sought out by newcomers who wanted to know the form. Was there anything going at Shaw Savill? When was the *Beaverbrae* signing on? And so forth.

But my money was running out and I was getting a bit desperate when one afternoon, quite by chance, as I was passing a ship in London Docks, I heard a great commotion breaking out on board. A few moments later an elderly-looking gent in spectacles, wearing a baggy brown suit and a soft felt hat, came clattering down the gangway with a suitcase on his shoulder. At the bottom he turned to shout a parting insult at someone on the deck above, then stumped off muttering to himself.

I've never been good at lightning decisions, but this looked like a sitter, so I started up the gangway – a bit gingerly at first, because I had no idea what I'd find up there. What I did find was a very fierce little man with bristling eyebrows and a strong Scottish accent – the Chief Steward.

'What d'ye want?' he barked.

'I thought there might be a job.'

'Ye did, did ye? Can ye strap up?'

That meant 'wash up', I found out afterwards, but I said 'Yes, sir' anyway.

'Can ye wait at table?'

Well, I'd been a fag in my time at Harrow, hadn't I? And I'd eaten at one or two good restaurants. Of course I could wait at table.

Mr McDermot looked me up and down. 'I want a lad who can work hard for twenty hours out of the twenty-four, see? And I'm taking no back answers, see? That's me. That's Tam McDermot. And the sooner ye and every other bugger knows it, the better, see?'

What I saw was that he was smarting under his recent failure to make the final crushing retort (which he'd probably just thought of) to the fellow who'd rushed off down the gangway. But all I said again was 'Yes, sir.'

Anyway, the ship was sailing on that very tide, so he took me on – as messroom steward. There was just time for me to collect my bag from the Red Ensign Club, join the union and sign on at the shipping office before it closed.

For no particular reason, except that it seemed the thing to do, I decided to change my name. So I appeared on the *Castelar's* articles as Simon Gray. And from then on, for the next two years, everyone called me Sam.

We sailed at midnight. First to Hamburg to load eggs for Santander – 1600 tons of them in crates – and various other tonnages of everyday necessities for different Spanish ports. I shared a cabin with the galley boy, a cheerful youth, a few years younger than me but a good deal wiser in the world's ways. In Hamburg we went ashore together after work; and since neither of us had any money, we couldn't get into much trouble – even strolling along San Pauli's Reeperbahn, where the girls leaned invitingly out of their horse-boxes, with the lower halves of their doors firmly bolted against obstreperous drunks.

We had enough coins in our pockets to buy a few beers, and in every cafe there was music and girls asking for drinks. We could only smile at them. And surprisingly they smiled back. I suppose that neither of us looked like much of a catch anyway.

To say that I settled down quickly and easily into my new life would be an exaggeration. I tried to do what I was told, but it was surprising – to Mr McDermot and to Percy, the second steward, as well as to myself – how much I had to be told. Little tricks like the easy way of drying a pile of plates (which I've never forgotten) or how to make a bunk bed in three deft movements, were as difficult to master as Latin irregular verbs. But much more interesting, of course. And I had to get used to being called Messroom, or sometimes just Mess! They'd yell 'Mess!!' and in I'd trundle. Maybe the soup was cold or 'Where d'you get this, Mess? D'you breed 'em out there?' and I'd have to take the plate away, flick the dead cockroach off and re-arrange the potatoes a little to make them look like a fresh helping. Nobody really cared, though. We had thousands of cockroaches aboard. They were thought to protect us from all other insects except mosquitoes, so apart from keeping the bread in sealed tins, we took no notice. I found it all most exhilarating. This was the life, I felt.

The skipper was a burly Welshman of about fifty. Mr Evans, the mate, was another, but younger. The other mate and both engineers were north country men. They got on well enough most of the time; but one day there was a fracas in the messroom – because the second engineer had taken too much salad, or something equally silly. I was astonished; I'd never seen grown men fighting. Even at school it couldn't really happen at meal times. But here they were, tangling like kids over the messroom table. In fact, the only losses were two plates and a tea cup, and next morning the Second's unpleasant greyish-yellow face was adorned with two quite picturesque patches of purple, but nobody seemed to care very much, one way or the other.

We spent the best part of two days in Hamburg, then back to London where the first person to come aboard for a chat with his friends, including the officers, was old Ned, the fellow whose job I'd taken. He was a great favourite, it appeared, even with Mr McDermot. Although he had looked elderly to me, he must have been about forty-two ... 'and not sharin' a berth with no bloody galley boy! The idea! At my time of life ... and a business man!'

That first evening Ned took me home to tea. He had known the *Castelar* and most of her company for several years and wanted 'to give the kid a few tips'. We took a bus to Plaistow and sat on top – me in my mauve gents' suiting (the only one I had) and Ned as he always was. Some said he wore the same clothes, hat and all, in bed.

He owned a tobacconist's shop, he told me. But every summer, for a month or two, he left his wife in charge and went off to find himself a ship bound for the Mediterranean – usually Spain. He was, nevertheless, a quiet and most abstemious man. The only gear he ever took with him was a steward's jacket and a suitcase filled with bars of Sunlight soap. I was intrigued by the soap and asked him what it was for.

'Well, you see, I got no vices,' he said very gravely. 'Don't drink, don't smoke, don't gamble ... But women! I love 'em ... and round the Spanish coast you can have any dona you want for a bar of Sunlight ... honest you can ... even me, and I'm no beauty ... am I now?'

He certainly wasn't. And yet he was one of the kindest men I met in those early days. I'm sure his wife thought so too. She was fat and cheerful and they had no children. Ned was all she had to look after. That was her life and she loved it.

It was she who bought all the Sunlight soap. 'He must have his clothes properly washed, and they'll do it for nothing if he brings them the soap.'

'They don't have any decent soap out there,' she added, rather severely I thought.

Our voyage round the Spanish and Portuguese coasts took about seven weeks, during which time I worked from early morning till late at night when at sea – sweeping, cleaning, waiting at table, polishing the brass, scrubbing floors – and I wasn't very good at it. But I battled on. And in between, there were wonderful Spanish ports like Seville, Valencia and Tarragona to wander through in the evenings; often alone, because the others usually made for the nearest water-front bar and stayed there.

We called at twelve Spanish, one French and two Portuguese ports in all. But I remember especially the narrow, cliff-sided entrance to Passajes; then the wide bay surrounded by hills and dotted with yacht sails at Santander; and Corunna with its Sir John Moore associations. And in Seville, miles inland up the Guadalquivir, through marshes inhabited by spoonbills and flocks of egrets, one magical evening stands alone. I had gone ashore late. It was almost dark when I wandered into the old town. The narrow mediaeval-looking streets were deserted except for occasional cats; and once a blind man, tapping his way with confidence from both walls, one after the other. I shrank into a doorway, but he knew I was there and called something to me as he passed.

A few yards further on, round a bend in the street, I came upon a real life Murillo – an open doorway into a softly lighted room, where a woman in a black mantilla was seated at her lace-making in the orange glow of an oil lamp. It was an unforgettable scene.

In Tarragona, with an afternoon off, I boarded a bus which took me several miles into the country. I started walking back and after a while caught up with some vaqueros moving a herd into town. One of them, leading a spare horse motioned me to mount. I vaulted onto its back and was immediately thankful that our instructor in the Cambridge cavalry squadron had made us do everything bareback as well as in the saddle.

This particular horse was a bit of a devil, and I could see that the grinning vaqueros knew this. What's more there was only one rein, but here again our instructor had taught us well; and in the end we reached a cafe on the outskirts of town in some style. The vaqueros bought me a beer, and I felt great. It was some minutes before I got back to reality. What I really needed to bring me down to earth was a loud shout of 'Mess!' But the vaqueros didn't know that.

Yet, even after nearly two months in the ship, I still hadn't come fully to terms with my new life – realised that it was soon to become my whole life. So it seemed quite natural, one day, to answer back when Mr Evans, the mate, complained about the quality of the cocoa I brought him at seven-thirty sharp every morning. I even offered to fight him, but that wasn't a success, and when we got back to London I had to leave, of course.

As the skipper put it:

'Can't have fightin'. Not in my ship.'

'They were fighting in Hamburg, sir.'

'Among themselves, you mean? Ah! That's different ... Look you, boy, Mr Evans is a gentleman, and gentlemen may fight if they care to ... If you were a gentleman, now ... Well, never mind. Here's your discharge book and your money ... Try to do better, look you ... and remember what I said.'

2.

Galley Slave

The winter of 1930/31 was bitterly cold. Tramping the pavements from Wapping to Millwall and on to Victoria and Albert Docks, I remembered the August heatwave of a few months before and how easy it had been, comparatively speaking, to find a berth in the *Castelar*. Not so easy to keep it, though; and now I was learning, learning with a vengeance, what seafaring can mean when there's a depression raging and ships are laid up, or sailing with reduced crews, as some of them did in those days.

At the Red Ensign club you could get a meal for one and threepence, and news about ships and jobs when there were any. It was the ninepence you had to pay for a bed that bothered us. We tried sleeping in a doss house at fivepence a night, but that wasn't worth the fourpence you saved. The beds were hard as boards – were boards, in fact – and all night long there'd be an endless clamour of drunks and metho-addicts; coming and going; fighting or snoring; yarning, arguing and getting nowhere.

What was much better, when it wasn't raining, was a bakehouse grating. There was one in the pavement at the top of Dock Street, where baking went on all night and the hot air rising through the bars kept two of us warm, while a third stood at the street corner on the look-out for patrolling coppers. Those where happy nights, talking or dozing with one's head on a sea bag against the wall and the entrancing smell of fresh bread pouring up over you from the basement cook-house below. We also found an eating place where you could get bread and dripping and a mug of tea for threepence, which made things easier.

But in January it froze and went on freezing. The wind came round into the north-east and blew a gale for day after day. That was bad, because I wasn't prepared for it with the right kind of clothes, or even an overcoat. I shall never forget the corner of Cable Street, which I had to pass every morning on my way to the Docks; the wind came whistling round there like powdered icicles.

Then I got a break. When I got back to Dock Street one afternoon, after my daily round of ships and shipping offices, there was old Tom, the bosun, waving a slip of paper with a look of genuine excitement on his face ... 'Here y'are, son; here's a job for you.' He took me out into the street again and pointed to a small doorway across the road. 'In there,' he said 'and don't come back till you've got it.'

I climbed a dingy flight of stairs to a door marked 'Ajax Shipping Company' – a somewhat pretentious title, as it turned out. Inside was an enormous man in a dark suit and light raincoat who, it seemed to me, entirely filled the little office. He was sitting on the corner of someone's desk; but what the owner of the desk looked like, or who he was, I couldn't tell you; the big man dominated the whole office. As I came in, he looked up sharply, his head on one side, biscuit-coloured, narrow-brimmed hat at a jaunty angle on his head.

I found out about that rakish hat later. It was a relic from the days when Victor Grantham had been a chief officer in the P & O. Now he was skipper of the queerest, raggedest little coaster imaginable, but he still clung to the grand manner. He sized me up at once. I could feel it, even though he went on to ask me a few stock questions.

'Can you cook?'

'Well, sir, I've done a bit of rough ...'

'Can you box the compass?'

I didn't know what he meant.

'H'm. What can you do? Eat, I suppose.'

There wasn't much doubt about that, and he could see there wasn't. 'Well, get your bag anyway. I'm sailing on tonight's tide. We'll get straight aboard.'

There followed one of the most extraordinary evenings I can remember. As soon as I got back with my bag, we set off up Dock Street, the skipper lurching along with such a roll (he had small feet, but enormous thighs) that we literally filled the whole pavement. In Aldgate he bulldozed his way through the late shopping crowds to a butcher's where we bought a haunch of beef, a leg of pork and another of mutton. After that there were groceries of all kinds, which had to be sought for in half a dozen different shops, including one where we also bought two enormous carpenter's tool-bags. With these crammed full of packets and tins, plus our three joints of meat, we boarded a District train going east from Aldgate, and about forty minutes later reached Dagenham.

There was no real station at Dagenham in those days, only two wooden platforms surrounded by an ocean of reeds – the Dagenham Marshes. We got out. The train flashed away with a cheerful clatter – bright and scarlet, fading quickly into the night and disappearing. It was as though life itself had abandoned us, leaving me with this monster of a man, in pitch darkness and the middle of nowhere.

'C'mon,' he said at once. His voice was high-pitched but confident and not unkindly, and there was something reassuring in the way he spoke.

We took up our loads and felt our way down some wooden steps on to the marsh. It appeared to be limitless, but we set off across it following a cinder track along the edge of a dyke – he loaded with groceries plus the legs of pork and mutton (there an invincible air of grandeur about the man), me carrying my bag with the haunch of beef on one shoulder. 'If Sheila saw me now', I thought ... and rather wished she could have.

Sheila was one of those extraordinary beings who refused to, or anyway didn't, fit into any particular mould. You couldn't call her a society girl, though she moved in the highest and smartest circles – in and out of them really. You couldn't say she was frivolous, though she was always laughing that chuckling laugh of hers; laughing at everything and everybody, including herself; perhaps more especially herself. And she wasn't exactly beautiful, though the light and the life in every curve and contour of her face, her laughing eyes, her coppery hair with greenish highlights, were something you could never forget.

We plodded on in a more or less southerly direction. It was drizzling now, as well as dark. The only lights visible were hazy with distance and probably came from ships out in the estuary. The wind had died and shifted into the south, so it wasn't really cold any more.

After a while the cinder track gave out. We squelched on through mud and reeds. My pointed yellow shoes (then very much in fashion) were soon soaked and oozing. I was bothered by the smell of blood and a trickle down the side of my neck, which I realised after a bit came from the beef on my shoulder. My collar went sodden with it and I knew there must be large and growing patches on the shoulder and back of my overcoat and my best mauve-grey suit. But I couldn't say anything, or rather I wouldn't have dared to; I wanted that job more than anything else. I knew almost by instinct that I could do it, and I would. I'd show 'em. By God, I'd show 'em. And as the words formed in my mind, I was sure I heard Sheila's chuckling laugh – a laugh of pure pleasure that made a joke of all pomposities, a laugh for sharing and enjoying.

Then the squeaking began. Ahead at first, but soon it was all round us. And here and there among the reeds we caught glimpses of little burning green eyes dodging about. Rats. They must have come from a line of enormous rubbish tips, like distant mountains, which loomed out of the darkness on our right. They were dumps of London refuse brought down river by barges to fill in the swamp and turn it into good building ground.

The rats must have been attracted by the smell of raw meat, and I wondered whether we were going to be attacked by hordes of them. But just then we reached the river bank, or rather the edge of a low earth cliff at a point where an iron ladder ran down onto the foreshore. At the foot of the ladder – a long way below, it seemed to me, but actually about 50 feet – lay the oddest little craft I'd ever seen.

She was some eighty feet long and brownish black all over – her sides, her deck, her superstructure, everything. Some of it was black or brown paint, of course; but mostly it was years of accumulated rust and grime. She was box-shaped and looked like an oversized coffin, pinched in at the ends; and her bottom I could see, by the way she sat bolt upright on the mud, must be nearly flat. Her name was *Woolbyrne*, and years ago, I was told, she'd been a lighter on the River Mersey.

I managed to get down the ladder clutching the rungs with one hand, my suitcase in the other, and the beef under my arm. In the galley – an iron deck-house amidships, just big enough for a rusty coal stove, a bench and a few lockers – I found a cheery Scandinavian-looking chap, whom Skipper Grantham called Harold.

'This is the new cook,' he announced.

'Cor,' said Harold. then more kindly, 'Well, what about some tea, then?'

I thought I'd better show willing. 'Shall I make scrambled eggs, sir? There's no bacon.'

'You don't call me "sir", cock. And I'll do the eggs. It'll be safer.' Harold, I discovered, was the chief engineer.

The skipper went out on deck looking anxious. I understood why when the mate appeared. He was tiny, but one of the most formidable-looking men imaginable. He gave warning of his approach with a loud clatter of wooden clogs on the iron deck outside. Then a leg appeared over the storm step, followed by a gnome's body and a gnarled white face with piercing eyes under a flat cap.

His name was Fred Whitehead, but that was less than half of it: he was painfully fastidious, a confirmed pessimist and, above all, conscious of an enormous intellectual superiority over all the rest of us, because a few years earlier he'd been in partnership with a mill owner in Belgium and spoke fluent colloquial French. He'd also married a very pretty Belgian girl (whom he brought aboard sometimes and watched like a hawk when any of us were around). He'd served in square-rigged sailing ships and we called him Mr Mate.

A loud clang as a boot hit the top of the storm step heralded the arrival of the second engineer. Frank never came fair through any doorway. He was a big, raw-boned lad, a bit younger than Harold, with rather fleshy lips through which he could blow the most excruciating raspberries. He was rough, kind-hearted and rather brash, yet sensitive. That sums him up, I think.

'There's no bacon for tea,' Harold announced.

'Who says so?'

'The cook says so.'

'Fuck the cook,' said Frank in a genial, downright sort of way. And forever after, that became a sort of Harold/Frank signature tune or battle cry ... 'It's going to rain. Who said so? The cook said so. Fuck the cook.'

Harold became my best friend. He was about six years older and very much wiser in the ways of the ship, the coast, the sea – in fact our whole world. And best of all, we were on the same wavelength – in thought and taste and sense of humour, as well as in practical matters. He could say 'No, Sambo, you can't do that' or 'Don't let them fool you, Sam' or '*I'll* tell the mate; he won't play games with me' and so on.

But they were great days, those eight or nine months in *Woolbyrne*, and they started right away. Harold and Frank were in charge of the two 100 h.p. Widdop diesels which, when they were both in working order at the same time, drove our little vessel along at a rousing 6.5 knots. That evening the tide was late, but about 10.00 p.m. we could feel some movement. Twenty minutes later the moorings went slack and she began to lift. 'C'mon, Sam' growled the mate. 'We'll get the springs aboard.'

It was the first order of a truly seafaring nature that I'd ever received, and I rose to it like a young salmon. To me that moment, as I leapt up the ladder to let go the back springs which were hitched to it, was the 'off'. Clichés like 'foot on the ladder', 'hand on the tiller', 'standing at the helm' jostled each other through my head, until a yell from the mate up forward sent them flying. 'What the 'ell 're you playin' at up there? Gawd 'elp us, Sam, you put me in mind of a nanny-goat with a toastin' fork!'

I flung the ropes down on deck and jumped after them. Harold and the mate let go aft and forward. The telegraph jangled. Frank opened the throttles, and away we went, out into the channel and on down river with both Mrs Widdops, as Harold like to call them, singing merrily and in unison.

The sea was calm and the sky had cleared. Vic Grantham called me up to the wheelhouse and began pointing out the lights which marked the various channels. 'You've got to learn 'em', he said 'every one of 'em, if you're going to be any use aboard here.' But really he wanted to chat – to find out a bit about me without asking any direct questions. You didn't ask chaps questions when they turned up out of nowhere – except about the ships they'd served in. But you could be curious. There was a sort of etiquette about the whole thing, which I'd learned on the queues and in the sailors' home. You kept chatting, and after a while a fellow would tell you what he felt like telling you, or maybe he wouldn't.

'How's your steering,' he asked conversationally after a bit, as though it were the most natural thing in the world for a youngster to do. I had a go, with moderate success. It was certainly a different proposition from the tiller of Marie-Ange Paitry's yawl, *La Marguérite*, which we used to sail in Brittany as boys; and different from my little bull-nosed Morris Cowley two-seater, love of my later school-days. But the principle was somewhere between the two, and I was beginning to get the hang of it when the mate came up and took over.

Out of *Woolbyrne's* total complement of five, four were officers, who kept the crew – me – hard at work and therefore happy. That was the formula anyway. But as a cook my skills were distinctly limited, so I bought myself a little book at Woolworths (it cost me three-pence, I remember) with the idea of adding a bit of variety to my menus. It was a mistake. Few working people appreciate variety in their meals, and the kind of variety that I could offer, after poring over my little book for an hour or so, was not always what was intended.

The trouble was that I couldn't make head nor tail of such instructions as 'season to taste', of 'place in a warm oven' or 'cook until done'. The high (low) point came when I tried to make Apple Charlotte 'by the book', and nobody got any dinner that day until I finally appeared in the messroom with a few sad little rusks – some brown, some black – at two in the afternoon.

'What's this?' asked Frank suspiciously, prodding at his with a fork.

'Apple Charlotte,' said Harold.

'Who says so?'

'The cook says so.'

'Well, Fuck the cook!' said Frank with great force, and followed this with one of his most ear-splitting raspberries, so that no-one should be in any doubt about his feelings.

3.

Slow Brown River

After that, the skipper decided to go on a diet. Not before time, I thought; he was too big to fit comfortably into the little messroom anyway. Harold and Frank reverted to eggs, bacon, sausages, cheese and tea, while every forenoon, about eleven, the mate would come stomping into the galley with a baleful look and a little cluster of cigarette tins (the round 'fifties' of those days) in which he had prepared meat pies, vegetables, puddings and so forth – each in a separate tin – to be put on the stove or in the oven ... *'and left there ... get me, Sam? ... Keep yer bleedin' 'ooks off me dinner, see?'*

So I became the ship's ordinary seaman more than the cook – or extraordinary seaman, as Frank would have it ... painting, cleaning, greasing, chipping rust (I chipped a hole right through into the engine room at one point and earned myself a long and poetic discourse from Frank and Harold), look-out, steering, handing warps and rowing the skipper ashore when we were anchored off. The mate was on my tail the whole time, hazing me from one job to another and never satisfied with anything I did. 'You'll never make a good seaman,' he used to growl. 'Make a good seaman cry, most likely.' But he never tired of teaching me, and I learned more plain honest seamanship in that little coaster than in any other ship I ever sailed in.

Between the mate and the skipper there was a silent but ceaseless rivalry. And yet they liked each other. The trouble, I discovered, was that they were both master mariners; but whereas the skipper had qualified in steam only, old Whitehead had been brought up in sail. And didn't he rub it in! 'They was men in them ships,' he used to snarl at us. 'They 'ad to be, and don't you forget it.'

But it was a wonderful life in a wonderful family atmosphere which you wouldn't find in any other type of ship. One trip, the mate's Belgian wife took passage with us, year-old baby and all. It was low tide when we berthed against the dock wall in Nieuport, towering twenty feet or more above us. An ordinary builder's ladder was kept on deck for such occasions. The mate set the foot of it firmly against a hatch coaming and his wife climbed up with the baby on her back and old Whitehead standing beetle-browed below to make sure that none of us young devils tried to look up her skirts.

The *Woolbyrne* was just a box really (Plate 1). She'd do six and a half knots flat out in a calm sea, and nothing at all as soon as the wind got up. If the tide was against us we had to anchor, or creep in and out through little known channels used by the sailing barges. There was a fascination about the slow brown reaches of the London River, especially in fog, feeling our way from buoy to buoy, with big ships' sirens blowing out in the fairway and bells clanging anxiously from vessels at anchor.

I remember especially one frosty night, with a full moon shining out of a hard clear sky and white mist lying in rolls across the mouth of the estuary. We were homeward bound from Antwerp, with the cook at the wheel and not worrying very much about navigation, when all at once a gleaming white line appeared out of the mist ahead. It glittered like diamonds in the moonlight, and for a few moments I watched it entranced. Then crash! The skipper burst into the wheelhouse and spun the helm hard over to starboard. 'Gawd help us, Sam,' he roared. 'Couldn't you see the surf? That was the Goodwins you were gawping at ... Lucky there was enough swell to make surf or we'd have been aground for good.'

But sometimes, when the tide was against us, we'd go aground deliberately. There was a bank called the Middle Sunk, far out at sea, where we used to dry out on a falling tide. Then we'd put our ladder over onto the sand for everyone to go cockling or digging for sand eels.

However, it wasn't always so deliberate; like when we stuck fast on the Margate sands one morning at high water. Fortunately it was on the outer edge of the bank that we took the ground. As the tide fell the old *Woolbyrne* lay back at a steeper and steeper angle, until she finally slid off stern first into deep water. Some fellows have all the luck; it was part of Vic Grantham's make-up and generally sunny temperament.

But I remember a rousing week in February when it blew so hard from the North East that poor old *Woolbyrne* couldn't get out of the London River at all. We struggled down almost to Southend, hugging the northern shore, then turned and ran for it, with a lolloping sea thumping into our broad little behind and bursting aboard. The skipper couldn't even get to his cabin, whose door faced aft, till at last we reached the Medway and scuttled into Queenborough, where we could anchor in safety.

It was bitterly cold. The decks got covered with ice, and after a few days we ran out of food, because even inside the harbour it was too rough to launch our boat. So all hands just got into their bunks and stayed there. Except me, of course; I was left blissfully in charge, and made the most of it – answering hails from passing coasters more seaworthy than we, semaphoring to the harbour office on the slightest pretext (to say good morning, to ask about the weather, even to check the time), and generally playing at sea captains all on my own.

Then one afternoon the wind died down a little, so I got the boat into the water and rowed ashore to buy some provisions. It was February 21st. I remember the date particularly, because when I got back aboard and unwrapped the meat I'd bought, I found that one blood-soaked sheet of paper was a page from the 'Illustrated London News' carrying photographs of recent society weddings, and one of them was Sheila's! It had taken place a few days before, at the height of the gale, and the picture showed bridegroom John bending down to control her veil as they came out of church. The caption underneath read 'He stoops to conquer' which, I believe, infuriated Sheila's poor mother.

It didn't annoy me. But the sight of that blood-soaked page did affect me more than I liked to admit, even to myself.

And now? Well, now I was free, wasn't I? Completely free to go where I liked and do whatever I chose. What I did no longer mattered to anyone else – except perhaps my parents. From now on I would be an actor without an audience or any critics. Except the mate, of course; it cheered me up to think that he, at least, minded what I did and how I did it.

On Whit Monday Mrs Grantham and her young sister joined us. We were bound for Antwerp, but when we passed Southend it looked so lively and full of holiday fun that the skipper decided to anchor close to the pier and let *Woolbyrne* dry out on the sands over low tide. We put the ladder down for everyone to walk ashore. Everyone except me that is. I was left in sole charge again, which suited me fine.

The mate had seen to it that I'd have plenty to do – squaring up the hold ready for our next cargo, splicing new lanyards onto some of our fenders, and so on. I became so engrossed in this that I lost all account of time – until all at once I felt the ship move and, at the same time, a thud against her side, then another and another.

I rushed up on deck, but too late. The ladder, which I'd forgotten to lash to the ship's rail, had been carried away, and was fast disappearing on the rising tide. I leapt into our boat, and went pulling down tide after it, for all I was worth – and got carried away myself. So when the shore party wanted to come off again, there was no boat, no ladder and no cook. They had to hire a motor boat, and I was left to struggle back towing the ladder. It took me nearly an hour, but taught me a lesson I could hardly have learned more thoroughly in any other way.

Part of that lesson, as I strove and struggled, gaining very slowly and with agonising effort against the tide, was the sight, on looking over my shoulder, of the mate's impassive countenance watching me ... just watching ... from *Woolbyrne's* stern. I was close enough now for a heaving line to reach me; but none came, and when I looked again he'd disappeared. All I could see was the bare, black side of the ship standing over me, completely void of anything to catch or hook onto. No ropes, no drain hole, no bolts – nothing.

I battled on in a series of infuriating jerks, as the ladder's rungs, acting like waterbrakes, stopped me dead again and again. I must keep the boat moving at all costs ... memories of Grassy Corner in the Cambridge bumping races, with me rowing 'two' in the Caius 3rd Lent boat, and John Pennington, our coach, yelling from the bank ... 'Up, two! ... Help her round! ... Pull, man, for God's sake! ... Bust yourself!'

There was no John Pennington now. And no bank. Only the broad brown estuary, with the flood tide sweeping up river. But I was busting myself alright. And at last, gaining! ... gaining very slowly. Soon I was almost up to *Woolbyrne's* stern.

But what could I do? If I stopped rowing, even for a moment, to reach up for the rail, we'd be swept away at once. I must go on rowing for all I was worth, and hope. I yelled and yelled, but nobody came.

Suddenly, I felt something rough and flexible against my back ... a mooring rope trailing in the water. I grabbed it and hung on, almost collapsed with exhaustion. And next minute the mate's head poked over the rail, looking stern as always. '... Who left that bloody mooring over the side? Was it you, Sam?'

I knew it hadn't been there when I last looked, a moment before: but I was too done up to answer.

Because of her shallow draft and flat bottom *Woolbyrne* traded to all sorts of out-of-the-way places that larger vessels couldn't reach. We used to run across to Belgium for bricks or cement, Holland for scrap iron (anything from car springs to old alarm clocks dropped into our hold by the ton from an enormous electro-magnet) or France for more bricks.

In and out of muddy creeks; along canals and through the centres of large cities like Bruges and Ghent, the sound of our engines echoing among ancient houses; waved to by girls from all the bridges, and by people eating at waterfront cafes. To almost unheard-of London River wharves from Greenhithe up to Brentford, and I remember one trip with a cargo of cowcake from Calais to Mistley, in Suffolk, where we had to quant ourselves with long poles alongside the ancient mill which Constable once painted.

It was a life of great variety and continual movement. And of course we knew all the other coasters of different kinds in the same trade as ourselves: the Dutchmen with their great high forecastles and poops, their decks so steeply sheered that it was a wonder anyone could stand up on them in a seaway. They were often manned by entire families, with wives as mates, sons as engineers, daughters cooking and usually a few small children. They lived aboard permanently. Their ship was their home. They decorated her with lace curtains and potted plants in the wheelhouse windows and all the skylights. There were cats in the saloon and usually a tree with candles at Christmas.

Then there were sailing barges, crewed by a man and a boy, tacking serenely up an East Coast river or the length of a Port-of-London dock. Two hundred or three hundred tonners they'd be; often with absurdly awkward loads, such as a whole hay-stack or half a pre-fab cottage. We used to meet them dredging up or down river – drifting on the tide with their anchors dragging to help them steer through the arches of all the bridges. It was an old barge skipper who taught me how to bake a curlew, feathers and all and coated thickly with mud, and showed me where the best mussels grew round the piles of a wooden jetty on the Isle of Grain.

There were several schooners, like the *Harwarden Castle*, a great three-masted 250-tonner, and the smaller *Henford*, both with crews of six or less to handle them. We all used to meet ashore – especially in the waterfront bars of Belgian ports, with great bowls of peeled hard-boiled eggs on the counter for anyone to help themselves, and Dutch family parties sitting silently at large round tables.

One of the bars was heated with portable oil stoves, which were an everlasting temptation to the mate of one of the schooners. He was another tiny man, but with a permanent grin on his great moon face. As soon as he got a bit drunk, he'd pick up one of the stoves and walk off with it down the quayside. Of course the girl behind the bar had to rush after him and drag him back (she was twice his size anyway). And no sooner had they come in through the door again, both clutching the stove handle, than the mate would let go and grab another stove by the handle – grinning and crooning to himself as he wandered off down the quay, for the whole performance to be repeated – perhaps three or four times. How the barmaid kept her temper was a perpetual mystery.

And there were girls. Of course there were girls. One of our favourites was Lulu (that really was her name). We found her in Dunkirk, in a café which was half brothel, or a brothel which was half café, we never did discover which. Anyway, it was a pleasant place to go for a drink in the evening and meet all our friends.

Lulu was a large girl of about twenty-four and rather fat in a puppyish kind of way, but always happy and smiling. At least I think she was happy, but she had a problem. She was going to marry the second mate of a freighter on the

River Plate run, as soon as either of them made enough money for her to stop 'work'. For him that meant getting the French equivalent of an Extra-Master's ticket and a good teaching job. For Lulu it was a more complex matter; she had a widowed mother, who'd recently had a stroke, and a young brother still at school. She didn't want to go upstairs with anyone and everyone, but her few 'réguliers' didn't bring in enough to get her out of the rut. So she had to be ready and willing at all times, but choosey.

That was where we, the coaster crews, came in. She kept a table for us close to the bar (her action station) where there was always a 'cassis' and an empty chair against the wall waiting for her if a drunk started being a nuisance. We never met her intended; he must have been a fine fellow from the way she spoke of him. She was an extraordinary girl, bubbling over with affection and good humour. I hope she made him a splendid wife. I'm sure she did, with her wide experience of all kinds of men and her way of facing up to adversity without letting it become a burden to others.

4.

Bricks Without Brandy

Occasionally we made quite long voyages. Down along the
south coast as far as Exeter, where a long rope attached to a
cart-horse on shore helped us round the bends in the canal
from Topsham Lock up into the heart of the city. Then up
the east coast to Manningtree, Ipswich, Lowestoft, and once
as far as Kings Lynn and Boston. But our principal trade
was to the Low Countries – Nieuport, Ostend, sometimes
Dunkirk, and back with cement or bricks.

Those brick cargoes were everyone's favourites. They
were easy to load and discharge; could be built well up in
the hatchways to make the ship sea-kindly and, best of all,
were ideal for hiding contraband. All you had to do was to
pull out a few bricks, to form a ready-made locker large
enough to take a good-sized packing case full of brandy,
cigarettes, cigars, scent and anything else that you or your
friends ashore might fancy. Then you'd build bricks back on
top, level with the rest (they had to be exactly level, of
course) and dispose of the surplus bricks elsewhere.

We usually had several of these caches dotted about the
cargo. The mate always had one of his own, which he would
set up during the night or when everyone was ashore; he was
a secretive old devil, aloof and taciturn. And wily – a deep
one, if ever there was, and one day after I'd been in the ship
a few weeks, I discovered just how deep he could be.

The Revenue boys knew we were smuggling alright, and
kept a watch on us. In fact they probably knew pretty
accurately what we were smuggling and when; because, of

course, they had their contacts over the other side and on every waterfront along the coast. But they bided their time, hoping no doubt to get a worthwhile haul one day – something more rewarding than a few tins of cigarettes and bottles of scent or brandy.

Then one afternoon, as we were chugging merrily up the Lower Hope towards Tilbury, they pounced. A launch came creaming out from Gravesend; slipped alongside, secured and put a keen young fellow in overalls and a peaked cap on board, all in one movement. His superiors – two of them – demanded to see the ship's papers. To get the skipper out of the way, I expect. He turned over the wheel to the mate and ushered them grandly into his cabin aft.

The young fellow turned to me. 'Open up the hatches,' he said sharply. I rolled back the hatch cloth of No.2 and started lifting out the boards one at a time. It was then that I got my first insight into the mate's true character. As I said, it was the practice to build up our brick cargoes in the hatchways for greater stability, leaving the space under my galley empty. We used this space as a sort of auxiliary bosun's store and gubbins repository; in fact, after we'd carried several brick or cement cargoes in a row, it was full of all sorts of junk and spare gear – old moorings, oil drums, damaged fenders, dan-buoys, lumps of drift wood ('that might come in handy; you never know') and God knows what else.

Well, when I opened up the hatch now, I was surprised to see that a few bricks at the fore end of the stack, next to the 'gubbins' store, seemed to have been lifted and put back in a hurry, awkwardly, so that they didn't quite fit. The Customs fellow noticed it at once. 'Right,' he said 'I think we'll start down here,' and then with an insolent grin up at old Fred Whitehead in the wheelhouse 'Any objections, Mr Mate?'.

For answer, the mate barked at me 'Get down there, Sam, and clear away some of them bricks and stuff, so the officer can see what he's doing.' Then to the Customs chap, trying to be helpful ... 'Maybe you'd like to have a look up forward, sir, while the lad's tidying up a bit.'

'No, I wouldn't!' You could see the chap's eyes gleaming. The mate said nothing, and I wondered. He never called anyone 'sir', never on any account, so I knew something must be up. Anyway, I went down and cleared a passage through the bricks into the midship space and would have gone in myself 'to tidy up a bit', but the customs searcher pulled me out of the way and dived in first.

'Come up here out of the road', the mate called gruffly, as the chap disappeared through the gap I had made; and for a long time we heard him crashing about down there with increasing fury. Then it sounded as though he was worming his way forward along the side of the brick stack into No.1 hold.

When I look back on it, I'm amazed at Fred Whitehead's monumental patience and restraint – steadiness under fire one might call it. After nearly ten minutes, he said quietly ... 'Put them bricks back, Sam ... I'll give you a hand.' He left the wheel to Harold, who had come up to the wheelhouse for a breather, and joined me in the hold.

We worked fast but in silence, brick by brick, taking care not to make a sound. When we'd finished Fred piled a few more on top and around, till there wasn't so much as a crack left between the bricks and the hatch coaming. Then we went aft.

The skipper's cabin door was open. Inside we saw him and the two Revenue officers with glasses in their hands, apparently on the best of terms.

'Has he finished?' asked Vic Grantham, with a lofty and all-embracing smile. 'Ask him to join us will you, Fred.'

The mate slipped away and was gone several minutes. When he came back he looked puzzled and a bit anxious ... 'Where's 'e got to, then? Thought I must've missed 'im and 'ed come aft 'ere.'

'What!' There was genuine alarm in the skipper's voice as

he struggled to his feet (it was always a bit of a struggle) and lumbered out on deck, making for the wheelhouse. The two Customs men got up off the spare bunk. The skipper took the wheel from Harold who went back down the engine room, and next moment we were swinging round under full port helm.

The telegraph clanged. The Widdops speeded up, and back we went down river at our full six and a half knots. 'Get a lifebelt handy!'. From the gallery I looked up and saw Vic Grantham leaning comfortably out of the wheelhouse window, one great fat forearm on the sill, and grinning like an old cat. Then I knew it was all a game.

But the Customs men, who'd gone forward with the mate, didn't. 'How could he have gone overboard?' I heard one of them say. 'He was down the hold, wasn't he?' But they looked anxious.

'No, he were in the forepeak, I think,' said Fred. 'He must've been through both holds long since.'

Then we heard it – a faint cry from somewhere. It sounded like a mixture of 'Hi', 'Oy' and 'Up', as though someone wanted, but hadn't quite the face, to shout 'Help!'. It came again and again, but was difficult to place. We scurried round, looking here and there – even overboard again.

It was one of the Customs men who suddenly said loudly and firmly 'He's down the hold, there. Bricked in. How the hell did that happen?'.

'Sam!' What the devil ... ?' roared the skipper. He *could* roar when he wanted to.

'Too bloody smart by half, that's what you are, Sam,' the mate observed acidly, raising his voice above the clatter of bricks as we dragged them out.

I tried to look crest-fallen. It seemed to be expected of me. But my act was completely upstaged by the expression on the face of young Bert, the Custom's searcher, as he clambered out on all fours, covered in dust and grime and grease from old moorings. He walked across the deck and straight over the side into the launch without a word or a look at anyone.

'Is he alright?' called the skipper.

'I dare say,' said the senior Revenue man dryly.

'Sam, get the decanter from my cabin.'

'We'll be getting along,' said the Revenue man. Then to his second officer 'Cast off aft'. He let go his forward mooring from our rail and took it on board with him.

'We'll be seeing you, then' called the skipper cheerily. 'Arr', said the Revenue as they sheered away.

It was a lovely morning, with a few skeins of mist still lingering over the meadows up river. The tall sides of tankers moored off Erith echoed our passing. On to Deptford ... past the lock gates at Surrey Docks ... then Cherry Gardens Pier ... Tower Bridge ... Billingsgate ... London Bridge. With the flood tide behind us we seemed to gallop on past the familiar landmarks.

But Skipper Grantham looked pensive. 'I didn't like that "Arr",' he said to the mate, 'didn't like it at all.'

'No' said Fred, but without much interest. We were all three in the wheelhouse approaching Hay's Wharf, when Vic Grantham suddenly made up his mind. 'I'm going to touch alongside here. Have a line ready to port.'

We swung round head to tide and sidled in to the wharf. It was deserted. Maybe it was already up for sale to developers. But the telephone box was still connected anyway. Vic Grantham was only in it for a couple of minutes, then back aboard and ... 'Dinner! Come on, Sam. We'll have it early.'

For the next hour I was kept pretty busy, so I didn't see much of what was going on. But several cases appeared from various parts of the ship – one from the engine room, I noticed, and a whole flock of bottles out of the fresh water tank on the galley roof. There were large tea chests too, from which the skipper, Harold and the mate took cartons and boxes of all sizes for re-packing into suitcases.

Then a car drew up at the wharf gates, which were locked. Mrs Grantham got out, and the suitcases were passed to her – over or under the gates. She had them into the car in no time, and drove away. What would have happened if a policeman had come along, I can't imagine. But none did. And as soon as we'd finished lunch, we chugged on up river to Brentford, which we reached about tea-time.

The wharf there is in one of the prettiest corners on the river – a channel protected by a wooded island, with the beer garden of the 'London Apprentice' at its mouth. It was right on high water when we arrived, so we went straight alongside. As we did so, a group of men in clean blue overalls came forward to take our lines. 'I thought as much,' said Vic Grantham, as he rang down 'Finished with Engines'.

They were all Customs men – six of them, and one to drive the crane. It took them till nearly midnight to discharge the cargo – leaving a bottom layer of loose bricks scattered around in both holds – just to learn us, I suppose. But Vic Grantham couldn't have been happier. 'By Jove! That was good of you,' he beamed in his most genial and expansive manner. 'Now you must come along aft – all of you – and have a drink.'

He gave them Napoleon brandy, but in a decanter of course. 'Can't drink good brandy out of the bottle. Can you?' he said pleasantly, 'like smoking cigars with the bands on.' The Customs men agreed. There weren't any hard feelings between us really; it was a friendly, if at times strenuous, war. But they must have noticed that the bands on the cigars old Grantham handed round later, in an expensive looking cigar case, had all been removed.

Part II
Away in Sail

5.

Squaring Up

Yes, they were happy days. But one morning we passed a Finnish square-rigger lying off Gravesend waiting for a pilot. We saw her again next day, locking into Millwall Docks. She was the barque *Killoran*, outward bound to Australia for grain, I was told. Of course I had to go aboard and ask for a job, and to my surprise Captain Karlson gave me a berth on the spot – as 'jungman' or seaman boy. She was sailing as soon as she came out of drydock in two days time.

When I went back and told Skipper Grantham – we were lying in St Katharine's Dock waiting for orders – he looked worried. I believe he'd come to look on himself as a sort of father to me, and in many ways he was. I didn't feel too happy myself when the time came to leave; the *Woolbyrne* had been my home and family for nearly a year. But old Fred Whitehead had been telling us all for so long that you couldn't call yourself a *real* seaman till you'd served in sail. So I put a bold face on it, and off I went.

It was noon on a Wednesday, I remember, when I went aboard, with a new suitcase which cost me thirty shillings, and a bulging sea bag on my shoulder. I paused at the head of the gangway, feeling eyes upon me from all directions – from aloft, where several lads were working in the rigging; from others painting and greasing about the deck. I went up to the cook lounging in his galley doorway amidships, with clouds of steam issuing all round him and powerful sizzling noises in the background. Dinner must have been about ready.

'Mr Mate?' I asked. He motioned me aft with a sideways nod of his head. I moved on down the deck and was passing the main hatch when a voice behind me – a warm, manly sort of voice – said 'Here, I'll give you a hand with that dunnage ... '

I put down my bags and looked round. A powerful fellow with a handsome, aristocratic face, very broad in the forehead, and serious brown eyes, was sitting beside the hatch coaming turning up a cringle from a strand of old rope. He got up, laid his work on the hatch and picked up my sea bag. 'Looking for the Chief Officer? He's down aft checking stores. Come along.'

That was how I first met Georg Londén, who was later to become my greatest friend of those first days in sail. For the present he struck me as a pleasant, well-spoken fellow, about my own height and age but enormously strong and clearly well-educated. If it hadn't been for his rather too correct forms of speech and rounded vowel sounds, I would have put him down as English born – the son of a country parson, maybe.*

We found the mate by No.3 hatch looking worried, with coils of rope, bolts of canvas, shackles and blocks and a vast array of paint pots piled all over the hatch. He was a grey-haired man of about 50, slightly built, with a pleasant apple-cheeked face and kindly eyes. His peaked cap had been pushed to the back of his head. He was shifting the stores about, alternately making notes on a pad and scratching his head with the butt of his pencil.

He was very preoccupied. Figuring was clearly a worry to him. 'Take the boy forward,' he said in Swedish, and turned back to his work.

We went forward to the forecastle – a large deckhouse

---

* I learned much later that his father had been a General of Cavalry in the Russian Imperial Army, and after the Revolution had commanded two Finnish cavalry regiments.

between the foremast and the main hatch, with a table down the middle and six bunks in pairs, upper and lower, on either side. A naked woman of exaggerated proportions was painted on the forward bulkhead. This was a tradition of some importance, because women in the abstract were one of the subjects on which men of all ages and races have most in common.

The galley was built onto the after end of the deckhouse, again with doors on either side – double doors (like the whores of San Pauli, the cook used to be told) which allowed him to dish up his hash without being invaded by hordes of ravening seamen.

Georg found me a lower bunk on the starboard side of the forecastle. We piled my stuff into it. 'Better wait till the hands come in to dinner before stowing anything,' he advised. 'These aren't my quarters. I berth in the half-deck aft.' Again I noticed the meticulous use of nautical English, and wondered.

Georg went back to his work and I wandered out on deck. Once more I felt those eyes on me – hammering that suddenly stopped, arrested movement aloft, a muttered conversation that ceased. But nobody spoke, so I stepped ashore and strolled along to the end of the dry dock, and stood under *Killoran's* bowsprit.

One's first sight of a square-rigger in her ugliest pose, squatting on blocks in the bottom of a drydock, supported by shores like a skewered chicken, can be daunting. The sheer bulk of the creature, her massive hull with almost square bilges, her bluff bow and the sharp angle of her forefoot – how could a few thousand square feet of canvas drive such a great pantechnicon through the water? On such a first sight of her, like a fat woman in her underclothes, you cannot know or feel how she will come to life at sea. Her heavy steel spars looked too clumsy to yield to the vagaries of wind and wave, on whom she must depend as allies and meet as foes.

Feeling very much alone, and perhaps for the first time actually lonely (even in one's first days at school there were four or five other new boys with whom to share the knocks) I shuffled back aboard.

'Hey! You come for dinner. Cont you like, eh?'

A young Finn with blonde hair *en brosse* and a positively beaming face was carrying two enormous mess tins of hash from the galley to the forecastle. 'Hey! Come.' He couldn't have been more welcoming. 'My name Saarinen – Pekka Saarinen.'

'I'm Sam Gray.'

'Hey, Sam! Come. Cont you like?' I never quite got to the bottom of this expression, which Saarinen found excruciatingly funny and repeated endlessly. It seemed to be a corruption of 'Country Life' and part of some joke of a vaguely improper nature, which he hadn't enough English to tell us.

The others looked up when we came into the forecastle. There were ten of them, varying in age from sixteen to about thirty, and one or two of the older ones introduced themselves. The hash, which they called 'Lapskaus', was excellent, and there was lime juice (unsweetened) to go with it. Then I put away a few of my things in half a locker allotted to me, stowed my suitcase under the bunk and my half-empty sea bag at the foot of my bed. My spare shirts and vests I tucked into a pillow case for a pillow. Then I was ready to start work.

I think the mate felt, at first, that I was bound to add to his worries and was rather resentful that the Captain had signed me on. He gave me a chipping hammer and a scraper and showed me some exceptionally rusty plating up under the forecastle head. I fell to on this; but about half an hour later, he sent for me. 'You splice this?' he asked, holding out the end of a two-inch steel wire rope and a thimble. I blessed old Whitehead, and got to work. I was lucky, and when you were lucky with those old flexible steel wires – when you got the angle of the strands just right – they'd melt into each other like butter.

That evening I went back to the *Woolbyrne*, which was still in St Katharine's, and went ashore with Frank and Harold for a drink; but I came back to *Killoran* early, and was asleep when the hands came aboard in various conditions of drunkenness. I was woken from time to time by someone flopping down onto the bench beside my bunk, sometimes more than one – arguing or singing or just chatting. In the end I got up and went out on deck.

It was a clear, still night with stars. Gazing aloft, it seemed to me that the masts looked taller, the spars slimmer and more elegant in the darkness. The quayside lights picked out the jackstays, blocks and other gear on the lower yards, but the higher ones were less clearly lighted and looked positively slender against the night sky. I remembered what old Fred Whitehead had told us: 'There's no danger aloft at sea so long as you keep a good hold – one hand for yourself and one for the owners, remember ... It's the rhythm that helps you ... the swing of her roll in a seaway ... same as the rock climbers (Fred was a Yorkshireman), they climb to a rhythm. Yes, it's seldom men fall at sea ... But in dock, when the ship's still, and especially when she's rock solid in dry dock, that's when you got to watch out ...'

Watch out or not, I felt a sudden urge to get up there out of the way and alone, away from the drunks and the din, away to think and be by myself. I climbed on to the rail by the fore rigging and up the lower shrouds, which were battened all the way up. The futtock shrouds and the foretop jutting out overhead were no problem. I knew about these from Fred; and looking down from the solid platform of the foretop I felt comfortable and at ease. For a while I stood there, then swung myself into the topmast shrouds, climbing the ratlines up to the cross trees, and was just going to haul myself over and up, when suddenly I froze.

To this day, I can't say why. It may have been the stillness, or the shore lights flickering in a puff of breeze, so that the rigging seemed to move but didn't, no rhythm. Whatever it was, I couldn't go on. I clung to those shrouds rigid with fear, unable to move an inch. And all at once a memory came to me, a childhood memory.

It was a memory of Cap Frehel, a rocky promontory, about three hundred feet high, on the north coast of Brittany. We'd sailed there in the fishing boat, *La Marguérite*, and looking up at those dark ironstone cliffs, inhabited by colonies of gulls, I suddenly got an urge to climb them. I was about twelve, and not a particularly brave boy, but like most healthy children I was always trying things.

It was a calm day. The cliffs rose from a rocky foreshore in clefts and ledges dotted with sea pinks and scabious, and the first fifty feet – which was as far as I could see – looked easy, so I began to climb.

It *was* easy, and by the time I'd covered those first fifty feet, I knew there was going to be nothing to it; one just had to go steadily on to reach the top in about ten minutes. The cliff bulged a bit, so I couldn't see very far above me; but there were good footholds and the ledges continued. On one of them I came face to face with a young herring gull sitting on a nest of sticks and fish bones. We gaped at each other for a moment. The stink was appalling. Then I climbed on ... and on ... and on. Before long I was out of breath, so on the next ledge I sat down with my back to the rock and looked down.

I wish I could describe that moment, but I find it almost impossible to put into words. Perhaps when you talk of bones turning to water you're about as near to the truth as you can get. Because in fact there just wasn't any 'down'. Below me there was nothing – only air – until far, far away – in another world, it seemed – *La Marguérite* lying like a toy at anchor. There was nothing

in between; the bulge of the cliff hid everything. If I'd
wanted to climb down, I wouldn't have known where to
feel for a foothold. And there was nothing above either,
except the next ten feet of rock face, then blue sky and a
puffy cloud floating lazily out to sea.

I sat petrified, unable to think coherently. Three lines
from Tennyson's poem about an eagle, which we'd done at
school the term before, went round and round in my head –
and have remained embedded in my mind ever since:

> The wrinkled sea beneath him crawls,
> He watches from his mountain walls
> And like a thunderbolt he falls.

I stared down at that wrinkled, crawling sea, and looked
right through it to patches of darker rock and seaweed, with
La Marguérite's anchor caught like a fish-hook amongst
them. A gull curved out on still wings and back again far,
far below. I closed my eyes hardly daring to breathe. It felt
as though even one deep breath would send me thunderbolt-
ing down.

And then, in a moment, it was all over. I managed to
collect enough courage to sit up, by the simple process of
flying into a rage – cursing and shouting at myself – and
was at last able to haul myself up to the next ledge. When I
poked my head over it, I saw a gentle grassy slope rising to
gorse bushes, and realised that I'd reached the top without
knowing it.

Well, it didn't all come back to me like that – as I've
told it. Clinging desperately to *Killoran's* fore topmast
shrouds, only that moment of panic and the wonderful
feeling of relief that followed were what I remembered. And
they did the trick. I climbed on up to the cross trees and
settled myself comfortably, with my back to the mast.

I felt at peace again, and ready for anything, just as I had
nine years before on the cliff top at Cap Frehel. The city

streets and buildings – dominated by St Paul's in those days – lay spread out before me. On one side the river curved round to Wapping and Tower Bridge; on the other to the Royal Docks, crowded with shipping and ablaze with lights where cargo was still being worked. I could pick out creeks and wharves we'd often used, and wondered if I'd ever see them again.

Had I made the right choice? Could any of the people in this ship become real friends like Harold and Vic Grantham? Yes, and the mate and Frank as well? I felt hopeful about Georg Londén, but how could one be sure? He was an apprentice, living in a separate cabin. Some sort of hierarchy was bound to be involved.

A whisper of wind stirred the rigging and set some halyards tapping, then died away. Outward bound. Outward bound for the colonies! But it was getting cold up there. I swung myself onto the shrouds and started down. When I reached the forecastle the drunks were all asleep, two of them on the deck. I crawled into my bunk and was soon asleep myself.

6.

A Multitude of Stars

We sailed next day. Or rather, we were towed down river by a Watkins tug and anchored at Gravesend to change pilots. After coffee in the afternoon, Georg called me out on deck. 'Someone's asking for you, Sam,' and there was little *Woolbryne* nudging alongside. Next moment a heaving line came whistling aboard. 'Haul up!' shouted the mate, and up came a case of oranges.

'From the skipper and his missus,' Fred called, 'And here, Sam. You'd better have this.'

'This' was a strange-looking spike – in fact a long rasping file with its edges turned up all along and the end beaten into a point. He poked it into the lay of the heaving line, and I hauled it up.

'It'll come in handy for splicing wire,' shouted Fred above the thump of *Woolbyrne's* engines as she chugged away down river.

'Fred's patent,' yelled Harold, who was standing beside him.

I still have Fred's patent spike, and occasionally I've used it. It wasn't a bad tool, ingenious in a way; the turned-up edges acted like rails to reduce the friction when you thrust it between the strands of a wire rope.

I kept in touch with Harold for a while, and I once got a letter from Fred with a Yorkshire postmark – just three or four lines asking where I'd got to. I replied straightaway, but never heard from him again. 'Gone shipmates ...' as Joseph Conrad once said ' ... are gone forever.'

In the morning we towed on down river and out to sea with a new pilot and a more powerful tug, which slipped us off the South Goodwin light vessel. The wind was northerly, but in the afternoon it backed to the south east and freshened.

By the time all sails were set (except the royals) and the yards trimmed, the wind had gone more southerly – a fine beam wind in comparatively sheltered water, with the French coast less than fifteen miles to windward. *Killoran* got into her stride, and all the doubts I'd ever had about the way she would sail were banished. She lay over, snoring gently and humming to herself as she slid through grey waters, her sails stiff with wind. White cliffs to starboard fell astern, grew hazy and vanished.

Watches were set, and I found myself on standby with four other lads. It wasn't till well on towards evening that I was sent to relieve the look-out on the forecastle head, and later to the wheel with an A.B. to keep an eye on me. He wasn't really needed; at a speed of 11–12 knots and steadied by the wind in her sails, *Killoran* seemed a good deal more responsive than old *Woolbyrne* had been.

At dusk the sky clouded over. The wind went round to south-east, freshening all the time. It began to rain, and we just had time to get our oilskins on before there were two whistles from aft to summon the watch, and it was 'Fore upper to'gallant!'

The sail was clewed up and five of us went aloft up the weather rigging to furl it. I remember Georg saying 'Come along, Sam' and shoving me ahead of him – just in case I needed any help or support, I suppose. But I was alright. To my joy it was exactly as Fred Whitehead had described. You swung to the roll of the ship, as though with a well-schooled dancing partner. And on the foot-rope under the yard it was the same; the rhythm continued and you felt completely at ease and safe. Clawing and heaving at the hard wet canvas was more exhilarating than anything else. Georg kept close in a companionable sort of way, not intruding but there. And the wind was warm. In our oilskins we sweated happily at our work. Then down on deck and up the main rigging for the same task there.

That first blow never came to anything, but it carried us well out into the Atlantic; and after casting about in calm weather for a few days in the latitude of the Azores, we finally found the North East Trades which sent us bowling down into the tropics in fine style. It was early September, so we had our older, lighter suit of sails bent on; and these would not be changed till we reached the horse-latitude calms of the South Atlantic.

One incident I remember well was the arrival on board, in about latitude 30°N, of groups of migrant birds – several different species, some of them not usually thought of as migrants, flying together. There were doves and green finches among the swallows, and a solitary thrush. And one evening a pair of small brown hawks, like kestrels, roosted in the rigging. They reminded me of the hawks of Bloemfontein, which I'd seen when touring South Africa with a schoolboy party three years before.

In the family we called them Aunt Addie's hawks, because many years ago my mother's great aunt, Adelaide McDowell, who was a missionary nun, had journeyed by ox-waggon to Bloemfontein – then a small mining settlement – and founded there the Convent of The Holy Family. One of her letters told of clouds of small brown hawks 'sweeping the evening sky in ecstasy at God's gift of flight.' I saw those hawks myself, wheeling and racing like swifts in the evening, when I went to tea at The Convent.

As *Killoran* approached the equator, the wind fell light and eventually died altogether in about latitude 3°N (Plate 2). These were the doldrums, that belt of calms between the North East and South East Trades, where the sun beats down onto an oily, glittering sea, and huge swells criss-crossing send the ship lurching in all directions.

Round the horizon squall clouds gathered. I have a picture in my mind of white plumes from a school of whales spouting against an inky curtain of cloud. The cloud growing upwards, to send grey streamers like claws across the sky. Then the rain hissing down over the sea and Pekka Saarinen, with a cake of soap strung round his neck but otherwise stark naked, furiously lathering himself as he rushed from sheets to braces and back with the rest of us; swinging the yards round, this way and that, to catch every puff of wind. Then hauling barrels to collect rainwater from spouts at the roof corners of all the deck houses, and running them aft on bights of old rope for skids, to be poured into our fresh water tanks through filler holes in the deck. Then back to sheets and braces. Haul and hold ... haul and hold. Now heeled over by a powerful gust, and tearing through the water to gain half a mile or so; now with sails flat aback and sternway on the ship; then round and on again.

Except for the mate, the crew were all young. Captain Karlson himself couldn't have been more than thirty-two. So this kind of exertion was almost a pleasure after two weeks or more in the North East trades, with yards trimmed to the inch, sheets and braces seldom started, and nothing to do but chip and paint and serve and sew under a burning sky. And in the calmer spells, in your watch below, you lay on the forecastle head staring over the side into blue-green depths, with the sun right overhead sending spears of light all round your shadow, striking deep into dark water with specks and flakes and tiny creatures darting through the rays, like dust through cathedral sunbeams. Dolphins lumbered by puffing and prancing. Sharks lay in the ship's shadow or cruised lazily around, tails weaving from side to side.

I remember especially one night of calm, with the ship rolling and sails slatting against the masts. It was pitch dark and warm. From time to time a hissing shower of rain passed over; then quiet again, except for the clatter of blocks and rigging as the ship rolled in the swell.

A single square of yellow light shone from the open door of the half-deck. I could hear a deep voice, Georg Londén's, reading in English from Conrad's tale about the ship *Narcissus*.

'She ran easily before a fair monsoon ... and moving along with her was heard the sustained and monotonous swishing of waves, mingled with the low voices of men ...

'A multitude of stars coming out into the clear night peopled the emptiness of the sky ... they glittered as if alive above the sea; they surrounded the running ship on all sides; more intense than the eyes of a staring crowd, and as inscrutable as the souls of men ...

'... the ship, a fragment detached from the earth, went on lonely and swift like a small planet .... A great circular solitude moved with her, ever changing and ever the same ... The sun looked upon her all day, and every morning rose with a burning round stare of undying curiosity ... '

I stood listening in the darkness, and those sonorous phrases flowing round me in the night seemed the most beautiful I'd ever heard. They brought a whole new meaning to life in a sailing ship; and more than that, a new understanding of the inner beauty, the rhythm, the flowing cadences of English prose in the hands of a master – who was himself a Pole. It was perhaps the same for Georg, a Swedish Finn (Plate 3); he could feel the inner beat of balanced phrases in another language.

After that – all the way down through the South-East Trades and into the Westerlies – we used to read Conrad together in the night watches, and it was through his writing that we both learned what Conrad himself called ' ... the power of the written word to make you hear, to make you feel and, before all, to make you see ... '

We became friends, Georg and I, as only long days of calm followed by trade winds in the South Atlantic, then gales with running mountains of sea in the Southern Ocean, can breed friendship – a friendship that never dies, nor changes, even if you never see each other again.

I caught a glimpse of Georg the following year in Mariehamn, when he was in *Viking* and I in *Olivebank*. And that was all. He was killed on the Russian front in Finland's winter war of 1939. But while we were together, we discovered something important to both of us – the true and enduring power of words to make you feel and see.

The South East Trades came to us in about latitude 1°N. The ship, lying with her head to the westward, turned slowly to meet them, leaning to their growing strength. A bow wave formed, extending slowly. The rigging sighed and went to sleep.

This was the start of two glorious weeks of brilliant weather – racing southwards, steering by the wind, with eased sheets and the clew of the main royal just lifting – the wind stiff and warm in your face and on your body. With the sun now behind us it was a joy to stand at the wheel, your eyes on the sails, or forward on look-out with the bow wave thundering and surging beneath you (Plate 6), flying fish spurting right and left, bonito and blue marlin leaping after them.

Up in the bowsprit netting some of the watch below dangled hooks baited with white cotton lures, which they kept dancing on the surface or just above it. Every now and then a great fish would leap and snap and be hauled up into the netting, then passed from hand to hand inboard.

At night, some brought their mattresses out onto the main hatch. There'd always be three or four talking or dozing or gazing up at the stars – Orion, the Pleiades, Altair, Arcturus and the Square of Pegasus – wheeling in slow procession through the basalt dome of the sky as the night wore on. They became our friends, beloved familiars watching over us while we yarned, discussed or argued the hours away, on every imaginable subject, simple or abstruse – on politics, religion, women, more women and the nature of life itself.

Somehow these were subjects on which we could all agree, or agree to disagree with equal certainty of the fundamental rightness of our own opinions. We analysed in great detail authors as diverse as Strindberg, Karl Marx and P.G. Wodehouse. We talked of music, poetry and the arts, the origins of the universe and again of women. There was always something to say about each, something controversial, charming, soul-stirring or infuriating. And the long, low swells running swiftly from horizon to horizon lifted us up and set us gently down with approving and companionable sighs.

Georg Londén usually joined us. But he was a strangely taciturn individual, speaking always in low tones with that deep and resonant voice which seemed to suit the gravity of his thoughts. He spoke deliberately, weighing every word and remaining for long periods silent in between. He seemed to carry with him a foretaste of destiny; you got the feeling that he had savoured life, found it inspiring and was now ready to move on into higher realms. As I write, I can almost feel him looking down on us with the grave and kindly smile we knew so well, and saying 'Well done, Sam. That's the way, old chap' (he loved that expression). And in my mind I'm on the main hatch again, looking up into the night sky, with long swells passing and our two mastheads, like twin skaters, weaving patterns among the stars.

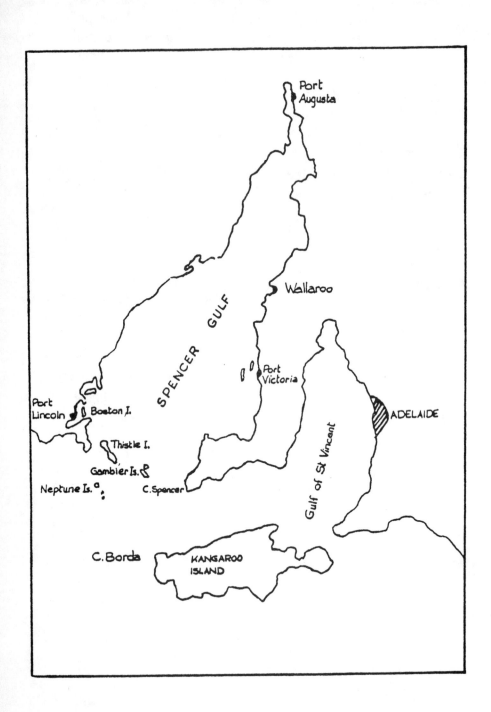

7.

Wheatlands Outback

About the latitude of Buenos Aires, the wind fell light and flukey, but the sky remained clear. Sails were changed – a prodigious task which occupied all hands for the best part of two days – and soon we began to feel a cross-swell from south-west, longer than the Trade wind swells from east-wards, but lower, which made *Killoran* stagger a bit in her roll.

The October moon was nearly full, and the sky still clear, when one night at the wheel I saw something which sends a tingle through you the first time you see it in any voyage: like a scimitar thrown by the Gods, an albatross sailed out of the darkness across the face of the moon and into our wake. This was the first time ever that I had seen one, and in silhouette in the moonlight it seemed to be invested with an almost magical grace – a faerie outrider of the west wind, wheeling and soaring against the night sky astern.

Soon the south-westerly swells were running higher, warn-ing of heavy weather, and a few days later it came, starting from the north-west with rain, which built up into a torrential downpour out of a long dark cloud. When this lifted, the wind flew round to south-west and freshened quickly.

Away went *Killoran* under what the bosun called her 'thicker warmer winter sails', and from then on she hardly paused all the way to Australia – some seven thousand sea miles in all – past Tristan da Cunha, which we left to the northward, with Gough Island south of us, then well south of the Cape, and on through the Southern Ocean.

This was a magnificent but testing run, for the ship as well as her company. Gales followed each other with seldom more than a day of calmer weather between; always starting from northward, then flying round to south-west and blowing hard for days on end. It was bitterly cold, and steely clear at night with ghostly beams of Aurora Australis fingering the southern sky.

Day after day *Killoran* raced on through a grey wilderness of tumbling seas, peopled only by birds and whales and the wandering albatross, with the giant brown-and-white striped Southern Ocean dolphins and sometimes larger whales to keep us company. Occasionally a big sea would curl aboard, but only the crest of it; with the ship in ballast, her freeboard was doubled, and she rode them like a cork.

Aloft, however, this gave us no reprieve. When sail had to be shortened it was usually 'all hands on deck', because we were down to topsails most of the time, and once we ran under lower topsails with a goose-winged foresail for two full days. They carried no reefing gear in those ships.

And yet, it was a stirring, almost uplifting experience. Except for your hands; the salt water sores, the split fingers and the cold (you couldn't work aloft in gloves) were a trial from which there no respite. But the comradeship, the absolute dependence, one on another, that was what made it all worthwhile. On the upper topsail yard in a strong gale, eight of you; maybe, on one yardarm, faced by a great billowing mountain of canvas, stiff with wind and hard as iron. At the cry of 'hold!', you'd all grab for it – fighting it, holding on for dear life. If one were to let go, the others might be flung down on deck or overboard. You had to hang on, and you did till you'd smothered the brute and all was secure.

Look-out at night was another testing time. You were muffled up, of course, in your warmest clothes, and here you could wear gloves; but even so, the cold crept in, and there was no shelter up there on the forecastle head ...

As we approached Australia, curving up from the south towards Adelaide and the Spencer Gulf, the weather grew warmer and calmer. It was getting on for mid-summer – actually the end of November – and we knew that once we got inside the Gulf it was going to be hot.

We anchored off Wallaroo, 85 days out from London; a smart passage for that class of vessel. The captain went ashore in the pilot boat for orders and next morning, when the sea breeze came in, about 11.00 a.m., we sailed on up to Port Augusta, at the extreme northern end of the Gulf, to load.

To say that it was hot up there would be an understatement. The thermometer had gone up to 120° Fahrenheit in the shade by 2.00 p.m. almost every day. But we weren't in the shade, we were in the sun most of the time – aloft sending down sails (and a month later bending them on again); painting the yards; tarring and greasing the rigging; repairing ratlines, and a hundred and one other not very exciting but very necessary jobs.

And there was nothing to do ashore in the evenings either. Port Augusta in those days was little more than a collection of wooden bungalows and small houses with red-painted corrugated iron roofs, each with its verandah, some of them overgrown with creeper, plus one or two saloons, surrounded by square mile after empty square mile of wheatlands and rocky desert country dotted with gum trees.

The Aussies were great. Wheat came down to the ship in two-hundredweight bags on trucks and waggons; but fitfully, a few loads at a time from the different farms and out-stations, and frequently none at all for a day or two. Gangs of stevedores (called lumpers) loafed in the shade, in or near the saloons, drinking beer, and when a truck or waggon came by, a few would jump aboard and come down to the ship with it.

They were a raucous, good humoured crowd – like the sulphur-crested cockatoos one saw around, both wild in the bush and on perches on the verandahs. But they worked hard, with a sort of suppressed fury, proud of their strength (one or two of them could lift a bag of wheat in one hand and hold it at arm's length) but contemptuous of almost everyone.

Yet kind-hearted to a fault. We were asked up to their homes every evening; to many different homes, though there wasn't a great deal of difference between them – one front lounge occupying the whole breadth of the building, with the verandah in front of it, and two or three bedrooms behind. The cook-house was often separate in a shack at the back. There'd sometimes be a bit of garden in front, with crimson or magenta bougainvillea trailing over the fence, but nothing much at the back – usually a dusty yard. Dogs roamed or scuffled in the dust. Perhaps a cat, and often a cocky (galah or sulphur-crest) on the verandah.

Harry was a great guy – a self appointed foreman of lumpers, perhaps because he had a louder voice than most of the others, or it may have been that the voice came with the job ... 'Carm on you f...in' layabouts, which bastard's next? Right! Get your f...in' arse onto that truck ... and you ... get f...in' moving ...' and so on. They loved it. It made them feel wanted. And so the work went on. And after work, home to tea at Harry's house, where his plumpish, smiling wife would be ready with a hot meal. It had to be hot, even with the thermometer at 100° or more.

Most evenings, Harry would take one or two of us home with him ... 'Carm on, you jokers ... Sam ... Pekka ... 'n see what the old woman's got for us ... I told 'er kippers, and I'll stop 'er cock ... I will ... I'll stop 'er cock fer a week, if it ain't kippers ...' The 'old woman' was a laughing lass of about thirty. And in fact she gave us sausages and beans, but I doubt if she suffered any deprivation on that account. Harry clearly adored her and she liked having his friends around. Sometimes on Saturdays or Sundays we'd all go out in the flivver – yes, a genuine 'T'-Model four-seater Ford – into the country.

At first the stark emptiness of mile upon mile of wheatlands, then mile after burning mile of rocky bush, was depressing. Nothing seemed to grow there but spindly scrub, with a few blue gums in dips and hollows or along the dried-up watercourses. Twisting dust storms – 'Williwaws' – moved across the landscape, one not far away from our track. The skeletons of trees, which had been 'ringed' to kill them and make room for wheat or grazing, lay about everywhere, or stood with withered branches like grey claws raised to the sky. Then maybe we'd come to a clump of taller trees and the ruins of what must once have been a farmstead – until the crop failed, or the farmer went bankrupt, or made his fortune at the races and moved into town.

In a country as vast as this, no-one bothered to clear away derelict buildings or machinery. You forgot about them and got on with the next job. Trailers, parts of harvesters, hoppers, bogies, all manner of agricultural scrap lay rusting under the trees, or tilted at crazy angles along the roadsides, making the whole area, with its jumble of tree-skeletons, look like a first world war battlefield.

We came across some aborigines – two old men and four women with children – squatting in the shade of a thorn bush. They stared at us unblinking, while flies crawled and buzzed about them. The half-eaten carcass of a large lizard hung from a branch of the thorn bush. Harry and his wife spoke to them in a kind of pidgin English which they seemed to understand; but they made no movement, and after a bit we drove on.

We were six weeks, almost to the day, in Port Augusta, loading three and a half thousand tons of wheat in bags. On January 12th we towed out into the Gulf, made sail, and found a bit of easterly wind, which carried us down almost to Cape Spencer, at the mouth of the Gulf, by the middle of the afternoon. The port watch spent all day battening down the hatches and securing each with a layer of heavy timbers, held down by strong-backs braced to eye-bolts in the deck beams. The starboard watch rigged lifelines fore and aft along the deck and between the fore and main shrouds on either side. The carpenter was busy making a sty under the forecastle head for the two black pigs we had shipped the day before.

At sunset a fresh breeze came to us off the land, and in less than a minute *Killoran* had gathered way and was striding ahead. Before it grew dark, we had left the Gulf and were making strongly into the south-east. The breeze freshened, the ship lay over. Water spouted up through the scupper holes and clouds of spray came hissing over the weather rail, till the decks seemed to be smoking. *Killoran* was a different ship now. She looked different – lower in the water. She felt different – slower to heel and recover. And she handled differently. Homeward bound!

The two mates stood side by side on the poop, watching the western end of Kangaroo Island fading astern. Both had passed that headland a dozen times or more, and once again they stood watching it in silence. At last the mate straightened his shoulders and turned to go below.

'That's Cape Borda,' he said, pointing.

'Aye! Aye!' said the second Mate, and went forward to the monkey island to check the course by standard compass.

The first watch of the voyage home had begun.

8.

Southern Ocean

For the next five or six days the winds remained light or moderate and the sea calm. But a long, low swell running in from westward slowly increased in height as we made our way steadily south and east towards the main stream of the West Wind Drift. The moon was nearly full and shining out of a clear but hazy sky. It gave a soft and silvery sheen to our sails. The long swells, muttering beneath us, lifted us along. Bow waves ran out bright and glistening on either side.

We passed the Auckland Islands, south of New Zealand, in latitude 49°50'S on the twelfth day out. That evening the sky clouded over, and by midnight we were running before a growing gale from west-nor-west, which continued for five full days – first north-west then south-west, then north-west and south-west again, with no respite in between. The ship sailed through it magnificently, but for us it was a testing time. For 36 hours, at the height of the blow, all hands were kept on deck, with hastily constructed strong-backs over the forecastle doors for fear of their being stove in by big seas boarding. When wind and sea abated a little and the glass was rising, one watch at a time went below, but had to sleep fully clothed in oilskins and seaboots.

They did sleep; one always does; but woke up stiff and damp to face the bitter cold of early morning and freezing nights. Sails torn or blown right out in the gale had to be sent down or repaired aloft. The pigsty was broken up by a big sea, which came aboard in the waist and ran forward when the ship's stern lifted to the next wave. It thundered in under the forecastle head with such force that we thought the pigs themselves must have been killed. But they weren't. Only angry. We had to drive them back with capstan bars and hold them at bay while the carpenter did his best to repair their sty.

My diary says:

January 22nd

We have had to abandon all future sugar-bug race meetings on the forecastle table, because the sugar-bugs have all turned into pretty little black beetles with white bellies and won't run an inch, even when encouraged by a lighted cigarette end. The weevils in the biscuits are just lazy. The rats hold themselves severely aloof in this weather; we hear them having concerts and tea parties in behind the forward lockers. Oh, and the cook having gone sick, the steward is making our pea soup and showing that he's forgotten nothing since he was a cook himself. He makes the most wonderful brew – thick and sweet, with carrots and onions in it, and great chunks of pork floating on top. You couldn't get soup like that at the Ritz, even if you offered to take it outside to eat it.

January 24th

At last, three weeks out from Port Augusta, comes a day of brilliant sunshine with a moderate breeze, giving everyone a chance to get all their gear out on deck. Mattresses, blankets, shirts, sweaters, sea bags, stockings, boots and shoes, everything is cleared out of the forecastle and strewn about on hatches, deck houses, lifeboats and the forecastle head or seized to lifelines and man-ropes to dry in the wind.

January 26th

A new hand who joined in Australia has cheered everyone up by making one of the classic howlers of the sea. It requires the combination of misty weather, the moon in its last quarter and a new hand on look-out.

Keeping his eyes conscientiously glued on the horizon ahead, he first sees a reddish glow which gradually increases in intensity, then suddenly changes into a tongue of fierce flame shooting upwards. He rushes to the ship's bell. 'Vessel afire! Port bow!' And next moment the upper horn of the rising moon has shot up out of the sea. The captain and the mate on watch continue to pace the poop with perhaps a grunt or a couple of words to show they've noticed. Everyone else, who's rushed on deck to find out what ship has been sighted, tumbles back into the forecastle to enjoy the joke.

January 28th

Today the wind flew round to south, and within the hour it was bitterly cold. We are down to 53°30'S already, so from now on we can expect hard cold days and bitter nights.

In one of the bunks, the portrait of a beautiful girl is pinned up with under it: 'The Hon. Gladys B., attractive daughter of Lord X,' and beside her on the bunk wall a plump completely naked French woman looking reproachfully at a lily. The society and girlie magazines hold an equal and everlasting fascination for these chaps.

February 15th

This north-westerly weather is comparatively warm. Of course, a lot of work at salty braces will split your fingers into deep gashes at the joints... and there's no remedy; when the skin becomes too hard and calloused, it splits open like India rubber and the salt water stops it from healing. Washing your hands in fresh water, whenever you can, helps a little.

February 21st

The carpenter has stowed himself away in his shop in rather the same spirit as a monk telling his rosary. He is just as deaf to the cries of the world and the devil, whom he recognises in the shape of the bosun forever roaring for the use of his (the carpenter's) workbench. When he can't get what he wants, the bosun falls back on his little forge, with which he makes harpoons, staysail hanks, hooks, bolts, bars and shackles.

February 26th

This afternoon the wind turned westerly again. By evening we had begun to shorten sail. When the watches were changed at midnight and again at 4.00 am., all hands were needed to get in a little on the weather braces. There are two men at the wheel now, with the ship making a steady 12-13 knots and big seas boarding on both sides. If this wind holds we'll cross the first of the iceberg tracks – the current which becomes the Humboldt Stream running up the West Coast of South America – before morning.

But it didn't hold. It fell calm. One of those breathless calms which happen from time to time on every voyage, even in high south latitudes. The night before, with a strong Westerly blowing, the sky had been clear, with stars blazing and Aurora Australis moving here and there over the southern horizon. Tonight calm, dead calm with mist closing in on us from above and all around. *Killoran* rolls helplessly in the long swells marching eastwards.

We are well south of the usual sailing ship track, close to the axis of the West Wind Drift – which separates all the main oceans from the colder, fresher waters of the Antarctic – waters full of marine life and the creatures which feed on it: whales, dolphins, albatross, skuas, Cape pigeons, ice birds and little black storm petrels, dabbling their feet in the water as they flick from wave-top to wave-top.

And tonight for the first time, the sad indignant cry of a penguin. The nearest land is a good thousand miles away or more. 'May be ice about,' the Mate says. 'Keep a bright look-out.'

The ship lies lifeless broadside to the swell, her bowsprit swinging over a wide arc of the northern sky. On the forecastle head, in the waist amidships and on the poop men stand in watchful attitudes, gazing into the mist to starboard – the direction in which the current must be carrying us. It's deadly still. The only sounds are the rush and gurgle of passing seas, the groaning of spars, and every now and then the scolding chatter from a company of albatross sitting on the water round us, waiting patiently for galley scraps. Once or twice we've seen the penguin porpoising among them.

It's hard to say when we first heard it, growing out of the night – a distant mutter and gaggle of sound, like people talking, but where it came from was difficult at first to tell. From somewhere to starboard anyway; with the ship yawing this way and that, one couldn't be more definite.

The Mate went to the standard compass. The skipper came up from below and joined him. The sound was louder now, and one heard an occasional squawk or cry. During my trick at the wheel, I tried to get a rough bearing over the face of the steering compass. The bearing didn't change. Whatever it was – a dead whale, maybe, with birds feeding on it, or floating wreckage – whatever it was, we were drifting straight towards it.

Everyone was on deck now: the skipper, both mates, the watch, the day men, even a few of the watch below – staring to starboard, trying to pierce the mist. Occasionally it lifted a little, and we fancied we glimpsed something solid out there. Once we saw ripples, but that was all. Then, quite suddenly, the bearing began to alter, passing down our starboard side and away. In a little while the sounds grew fainter. By the time my hour at the wheel was up, they were gone and there was silence again, a brooding silence. Till just before dawn the wind came in from northward and *Killoran* filled away for Drake's passage and the South Atlantic.

It had been an eerie experience. What was it that we passed

in the night? If it was something just floating, we'd both have been drifting at the same speed over the windless sea. Maybe it was a shoal of fish, or some dying creature, preyed on while still alive by birds or other creatures ferocious for food in those icy regions. We pondered and argued about it for a few days, and then forgot it in the sun, the bright seas and the thrumming of a full trade wind in our rigging, as we bowled up the Atlantic for Europe and home.

It wasn't until five or six years later, in a different ship and very different weather, that I thought of that night again. The barquentine *Cap Pilar* was working down the west coast of Santa Cruz, one of the Galapagos Islands. It was bright, clear weather, but soon after sunset the wind fell away and we were left drifting in a strong south-going current. The only obstacle between us and open water was Nameless Island, a solitary pinnacle of rock 300 feet high, black and forbidding in the darkness and directly in our path. It was impossible to tell how far off it was. All we could do was to watch its bearing on both compasses.

The bearing didn't change. We were driving straight towards it. And soon we could hear the booming of surf and seals barking. It looked as though in ten minutes or less we'd be smashed helplessly against the base of those towering cliffs. When all at once the bearing began to alter: the current had divided, as of course it must, and a few minutes later we'd been swept round the eastern side of Nameless I. into clear water beyond.

The experience set me thinking again of that night in the Southern Ocean, nearly six years before. I realised now that the same thing must have happened. We almost certainly passed an iceberg, with seven eighths of its mass submerged and reaching down into slower water – or perhaps even an eddy, they occur in all the ocean currents – which held it up against the surface drift carrying us eastwards at about one knot. We were lucky that night to be in the grip of the West

Wind Drift with no wind, so that we were swept helplessly round that berg. If we'd been sailing in a lively sea, we might have hit it without ever hearing the birds or anything else before we struck. I wonder how many ships, who disappeared without trace between Australia and the Horn, have done just that?

March 4th

This morning we raised Diego Ramirez, those two great pinnacles of rock – solitary outposts of Cape Horn – which stand in the open ocean in Lat. 56°28'S, Long. 68°43'W. It's going to be a long voyage, probably longer than anyone on board, including the officers, can remember.

Just before day-break the wind began to freshen, and by mid-morning it was blowing a gale with heavy rain from west-nor-west. We shortened sail throughout the forenoon, and when the watches were changed at one o'clock we were down to topsails and foresail only. She seemed to be running fairly comfortably at 11-12 knots when the port watch went to dinner; but we hadn't got more than a few mouthfuls into us before the old three whistles came from aft and we had to turn out again. It was going to be 'watch on ... stop on ... ' for the next day or two; we could read the signs.

We live in our oilskins these days, lashed with tarred spunyarn round wrists and the tops of seaboats. If this is done properly, and extra tar sloshed around the joints before the lashings are put on, you stand a good chance of keeping fairly dry and warm. When big seas come aboard and wash you about (Plate 4), it takes a little time for the water to penetrate, and with luck (if you aren't hanging on to something vital that can't be left, like a brace or a sheet) you'll be able to leap for the lifeline and haul yourself clear before any water can really seek in and soak you. But once the lashings are on and well payed with Stockholm tar (sailor's blood, fooken!), they have to stay there. Some, including myself, haven't had our clothes off for a couple of weeks, and don't expect to take them off till we're north of the Falkland Islands.

When we came on deck, it was blowing a full gale with driving rain and spray. It pinned one to the weather shrouds in the fiercer gusts, as we struggled aloft to the main upper topsail yard, which had already been lowered and the sail clewed up. It took twelve of us to subdue those great bags of canvas, stiff with wind; and no sooner had we got down on deck than it was 'In Foresail!' and the battle had to begin all over again.

It was an even fiercer battle on the fore yard. Both watches, the second mate and the day men – bosun, sailmaker and carpenter – were needed to furl the foresail. By now the decks were awash, every second wave coming green over the lee rail, and sometimes, when she rolled to windward, over the weather rail as well.

With the sea still rising and no foresail to keep her head away before the wind, *Killoran* had become very heavy to steer, even with two men at the wheel and the mate on watch keeping handy in case a third were needed. From time to time in the squalls, big seas running in on the port quarter would catch her awkwardly and threaten to broach her to. Then the mate and both helmsmen had to strive like demons to get another half turn on the wheel and keep her head away; and once she started to pay off, it was just as vital to meet her before she went too far. And so she ran on through the afternoon and into the night.

March 5th

At dawn the wind seemed to take off a bit, backing more westerly, and it stopped raining. But the respite was brief. A dark bank of cloud came racing up astern, with white water under it and a flash or two of lightning. Next moment it was howling over us. The mate fought his way to the fore upper topsail halyards, the second mate and bosun to the sheets; the rest of us manned clewlines and buntlines. But we were

too late. With an almighty   llowed by
thundering of torn canvas, th   ut of its bolt
ropes and disappeared in tags   ward. The rain
drove over us in sheets. For an   inute (it felt like
hours) the ship cowered, heeling   starboard, as the
helmsmen, helped by the skipper,   tled to keep her head
away. Then she struggled up and ra on.

But the worst was over. There was a lightening of the sky
astern and soon the horizon emerged, as the skirts of the
squall cloud lifted. A little while later the wind backed to
West-South-West, still blowing hard but with less vice in it.
The yards were trimmed, and all through the forenoon the
wind steadily decreased. By noon it was no longer necessary
to keep two men at the wheel, though the sea was still
running high, and a bit confused with the change of wind.

It was my trick from twelve to one. It's always an
anxious time when the extra man is taken from the wheel
after a blow. Though wind and sea are decreasing, every
now and then a big fellow will come thundering after you
with an extra turn of speed and maybe catch the ship on the
quarter, when she no longer has the steadying influence of a
stiff breeze and good way on her to give power to her
rudder. The watch will probably be at the braces, trimming
the yards to meet the new conditions. If the big one comes
aboard suddenly and the helmsman is caught napping, there'll
be trouble and may be damage to men as well as to the ship.

March 7th
Before evening the sky had cleared, and there was the full
moon again – for the third time in the voyage. The steward
came forward with the rum bottle and doled out a tot for
everyone, except those who didn't drink – there were two of
them, one an able seaman.

Fifty-five days to the Horn. Is that a record, we wonder?
It's certainly the slowest passage through the Southern Ocean
that anyone can remember. But we're into the Atlantic at

last, so th   The wind has come round to
south-south-   cleared, and it's bitterly cold
again; but at   nd, and if it holds we should
be past the F   standing north into warmer
weather within a fe

9.

Seeing Things

March 12th

For the past two days a large black bird with a face like Beelzebub has haunted the ship – sometimes floating a few feet above the heads of men working aloft; occasionally perching on the main truck and sitting there with its head under its wing. Once the second mate shouted at it. It turned a face contorted with hate towards him, spat over its shoulder, then put its head back under its wing and refused to take any more notice.

March 14th

Although the wind has gone northerly, it's still very cold. We're keeping a bright look-out for ice because we're now in another current which brings bergs and growlers up from the Antarctic – sometimes almost as far as the River Plate.

The sea is full of krill, and for the past two days we've had penguins 'skrarking' round the ship all night, playing and fishing by day. This morning a school of large silver-sided dolphins were with us for an hour or two; but the carpenter hasn't yet fitted a new shaft to our harpoon, so nobody bothered them. Just after dark they came back. You could see them under the bowsprit – great trails of phosphorescent light waving from side to side, like tentacles of a giant octopus or space rockets gone mad.

March 18th (Lat. 39°40'S Long. 29°20'W)

About the middle of the forenoon the sea round the ship

suddenly went a muddy brown, and when we looked over the rail we saw that we were sailing through what looked like a square mile of semolina and chicken broth. The draw bucket was dropped over, and we found that we were in a sea of squid larvae – little egg-shaped transparent bodies with dainty brown and white fringes at one end. The albatross and penguins who left us nearly a week ago are missing a 'fancy gorge', and no mistake.

March 28th (Lat. 28°31'S Long. 25°31'W)
During my hour at the wheel in the forenoon watch I was mystified by some queer little puffs of cloud which appeared quite suddenly in the sky to leeward. The first was a small white crescent like a sickle moon, that changed shape rapidly although there was little perceptible movement in any of the other clouds. Then, against a background of high white stratus, there appeared two more little puffs, quite black, which also changed shape quickly. After a while they all disappeared as suddenly as they had come. There were no aircraft about, or warships who might have been firing anti-aircraft guns, so what on earth had we seen?

Perhaps one ought not to ask. There was the summer evening at my grandfather's home in Sussex – I was about five at the time – when I suddenly noticed that the rabbits scampering up and down a hedgerow on the other side of a four-acre meadow were playing football with an oak-apple.

I sat and watched them for several minutes. I could see every move. The oak-apple bounded from one to the other in the slanting sunlight, and I remember feeling worried because a reddish patch in the hedgerow looked like a fox watching them too. But I knew it wasn't. I knew, and clearly remember knowing, that I was imagining the fox. But not the football game, that went merrily on until at last I couldn't bear to keep it to myself any longer, and rushed off to fetch our Belgian governess.

Of course, when I got back with her, the game had stopped. The rabbits were still there, lolloping about or feeding, but they'd stopped playing football, and never did again, though I watched every evening till we left for home a week later. And yet I've never doubted for a moment that I saw what I saw – even though my governess took the trouble to go to the other side of the meadow and hold up an oak-apple, just to show me that it couldn't in fact be seen at that distance.

Of course it couldn't – not an ordinary oak-apple on an ordinary evening. And obviously if, in some magical way, I'd seen the rabbits playing football, it wouldn't be any more difficult to see them playing it on their hind legs, kicking an oak-apple – even at a range of two hundred yards or so.

In fact, I think we miss far too many chances of understanding the true nature of things by always trying to link what we see or feel with what can be proved to be there. A year or two ago, a woman I know began to describe how one night, while driving over the Dorset hills, she'd suddenly noticed a large cigar-shaped object with rows of lighted port-holes hanging motionless in the sky above Lyme Regis. She watched it carefully, and after a while it began to move slowly away. Then it increased speed, and finally shot up into the heavens and disappeared.

When she'd finished telling us about it I started to suggest explanations, the way one does – the beam of a search light striking a filmy layer of cloud; a ship at sea looking as though it were floating in the sky, due to a misty horizon, and so on. Till suddenly her husband interrupted, 'You know,' he said, 'you're on the wrong tack altogether ... What Marjory's been telling you is that she *saw* a flying saucer. That's the only *fact* about the whole incident: she *saw* a flying saucer. Anything else – any attempt to explain what was there – is pure conjecture and therefore unimportant.'

And so it was, when you think about it. In the limited state of our knowledge, you're just as likely to miss a vital truth by trying to make what you see fit the known facts, as you are by leaving your mind open to the possibility of new and unheard-of facts, which might one day match up with what you saw.

Of course, sometimes you just *have* to check. If you're on look-out in a ship at night and you see orange flames leaping out of the sea ahead, its worth waiting a moment before turning out all hands, just to make sure it isn't the upper limb of the moon rising out of haze on the horizon. And in the tropics there are mirages, and volcanic islands which appear and disappear – even floating islands, broken off some headland in Antarctica by ice pressure and carried far out to sea on a drifting berg.

If you're a seaman you have to investigate such phenomena. But there are other times when, if you're too analytical, you'll throw away the chance, which may come only once in a lifetime, of discovering something far more important about the universe than hard facts. If you're lucky enough to recognise these chances, you should hang on to every moment of seeing, feeling, hearing. If you go and fetch your Belgian governess, you've had it.

March 30th

During the afternoon of March 30th a heavy black squall came by, but not close enough for us to collect any water. Above its dark skirt of falling rain, great boulders of cumulus clambered over each other. At sunset they were tinged with ink and orange. Then, as the sky grew dark, sheet lightning blazed from behind them, throwing the clouds into black relief. Our fresh water tanks are getting low; we need a heavy rain squall, and soon.

April 3rd (Lat. 21°24'S Long. 34°26'W)

Rain at last. We were at it all through the middle watch this morning, collecting water from the poop and the deck houses into barrels, which we then ran up or down the deck on a bight of old rope. The rain came down in a proper tropical downpour. We splashed about revelling in the soft warm water.

Rain! Rain! Rain! A sudden burst of scorching sunshine between the clouds, then rain again. We very soon filled all our water tanks, but still the bulging rain clouds with skirts of black velvet came crowding one after another over the eastern horizon. On great grey legs and pillars of teeming rain they came marching down upon us, the sea boiling and hissing beneath them or whipped by gusts of wind. Sea and sky would disappear and the ship lie with slatting sails under cataracts of soft warm water, pouring down almost solid and rising again in a thick mist, till it was difficult even to breathe in comfort.

April 10th (Lat. 3°45'S Long. 32°15'W)
Land ho! The watch below tumbles out on deck and there, not ten miles to leeward and nearly abeam are the towering crags of Fernando Noronha off the North East corner of Brazil. A pencil of lava about 1,000 feet high – the weathered core of an ancient volcano – rises out of the middle of the island. It stands like a great cathedral among the mountains; and far below, by the water's edge, we can see the white houses of a small village. What a wonderful position – on the weather side of the island with everlasting Trade winds coming in from the sea. And between 2.00 and 3.00 p.m. – the hottest part of the day – the sun has already dipped behind those high mountains, leaving the village in shadow.

April 14th
Yesterday evening the sky cleared and this morning we were becalmed. Soon there were sharks around us, and by noon we had four on deck, plus one to whose tail they tied a lump of timber and cast him loose again – to be attacked and eaten by his mates, no doubt.

The Mate is convinced that catching sharks brings favourable winds, and sure enough by the middle of the afternoon we were making 3-4 knots on a freshening north-easter – the first breath of the North East Trades for sure. 'If we'd kept that fifth shark aboard, we'd have been doing 6 knots,' growled the mate. There must be a moral in that. Perhaps many.

April 18th (Lat. 18°40'N Long. 46°59'W)

We're a long way west of the usual sailing ship track, and still nearly 2,000 miles from home. This morning small patches of Sargasso weed floated by, and these grew larger and more frequent as the day wore on.

Sailing at only 2-3 knots, we can sometimes catch clumps of weed and bring them aboard, complete with the tiny crabs and marine insects which inhabit them. You can see these crabs scuttling at high speed from patch to patch across the surface of the sea, and in some parts of the ocean there'll be sea snakes as well – all of them deadly poisonous, by the way.

A school of bottle-nosed whales were playing round one of the larger patches of weed, with half a dozen terns circling above them screeching.

April 30th

This morning we started changing sails, from the fair weather suit which we bent on when we passed the tropic of Capricorn more than a month ago. At dinner time we were astonished and indignant to find that all the meat and fish on board had run out (or so the cook told us) and we'd have to make do with pancakes and marmalade for the rest of the voyage!

This was horrifying, but there was nothing to be done about it. You can't go on strike in a sailing ship at sea; not only would it be classed as mutiny, but it couldn't possibly get you anywhere. And getting somewhere – home to Europe – was all we really cared about just now.

The wind fell light again, but remained easterly and on May 2nd we sighted Fayal, westernmost of the Azores. Our spirits rose.

10.

A Taste of Home

Our arrival off Falmouth on May 16th marked the end of a 133-day voyage from the Spencer Gulf – one of the longest for many years. Nevertheless, no-one went ashore, because orders were brought out to the ship by harbour launch to proceed direct to Sunderland to discharge. And since the wind was westerly and remained so for the next two days, then backed to south-east and freshened, we had no difficulty in reaching the Tyne on May 22nd.

As soon as we were berthed, I went aft and asked to see Captain Karlson. He was in a cheery mood, with bottles on the cabin table and the mate, the man from Clarkson's (our agents), the tug skipper and another fellow, whom I took to be the ship's chandler, sitting round it.

'You go back to be gentleman again, Gray?'

'No. But I'd like to have a week or two at home.'

He gave me the pay I'd earned to date, which I think was about twelve pounds. And that night I caught a long distance bus. I remember the soft lighting all night and the oh-so-comfortable seats with high backs. One felt cocooned and cradled, gazing out at the softly rolling Yorkshire country-side. A pretty stewardess spoke to me, but I was slow to answer, because my reply came naturally into my head in Swedish and had to be translated. She must have thought me dull and stupid. Anyway I was left alone after that and slept for most of the journey.

My father was pleased to see me. I think he'd given me up as something of a lost cause, and had to re-adjust to the idea that I was actually getting to grips with life and embarking on a career at last, even if an unconventional one not likely to be very profitable. After all, he'd done the same himself, leaving Harrow at the age of sixteen to read natural sciences at Heidelberg University, where he got a good degree, and later a Ph.D. at Zurich. I was going to do something similar at sea, he understood, and meantime the Aluminium Plant and Vessel Company, which he'd founded in 1910, the year after I was born, required his full attention.

This sounds as though my welcome home was a somewhat low key affair. And so it was, on the surface. But fifty years later one of my brothers told me that from the day I left (after breakfast on July 18th, 1930), the small side door at Lincoln House, Parkside, Wimbledon Common, was never again locked ... just in case. A ritual was established, which never varied: every night at ten, my father went his rounds, making sure that all the ground floor windows were secured and all outside doors locked and bolted (there were seven at Lincoln House), except for that small side-door, screened by the rhododendrons in our driveway. My father opened and closed it every evening, to make sure it wasn't stuck or anything ... just in case.

My mother was full of enthusiasm for everything I told her about my adventures and my plans for the future. She had always had a romantic attachment to 'little inns'. For her there were no such things as bars or brothels or public houses; only little inns where sailors and pirates congregated and sang songs. She was, nevertheless, a talented writer, artist and sculptor – skills she inherited from both her father and her mother – and a great organiser of 'worthwhile' projects.

One such project provided mobile medical units, called Skippo vans (Skippo was a mountain goat of her imagining) to tour the remoter villages of India. Then there was the 'Second Wednesday Lunch Club,' founded in the days when she had been an active campaigner for the Liberal Party. My

mother and her friends offered active support for Mahatma
Ghandi when he came over (her faithful chauffeur, Fred
Fletcher, was distressed and couldn't think what to do with
the car rug when the holy man insisted on sitting crossed-
legged on the floor in the back of the Rolls). And a few
years later, even greater efforts were made to ensure a
worthy welcome for Haile Selassie and his entourage, despite
strenuous efforts by the government of the day to keep him
at arm's length for fear of offending Mussolini.

My sister was now married to an Oxford professor. My
brothers were at prep school, Harrow or Cambridge. In
fact there were great doings and comings and goings in
every quarter and after a very few days I felt over-
whelmed by both the level and the intensity of all these
activities. I had lost the knack and the taste for great
events and their protagonists.

I went to see Sheila. She and John now lived in a flat in
Craven Gardens. John was at work when I called one
afternoon, but Sheila made tea, and there was the usual
gurgle of amusement as I tried to balance a delicate cup and
saucer and a plate on knees more accustomed now to being
braced between yard and jackstay, fighting canvas.

I asked after one or two people we'd often talked about,
people she knew well but I'd only just met. 'How about
Patrick Kinross?'

'He got married to Bridget in the end.'

'And that Hastings girl, wasn't she a bit of a problem?'

'Oh, she thinks she's rather grand – being a bridesmaid at
the Kinross wedding. She brought some of the others to tea
after it and was on about what I'd done with my life ... You
know, what had I achieved and all that ... And Pen Cunard
said "Well, *you* haven't got a man rolling round the Horn
for you!"'

'Oh, dear. Was she cross?'

'Not really, I don't think she believed it ... It isn't really
true anyway, is it?'

'Actually, yes ... Still I don't think either of us'll regret it. Do you?'

All I got out of that was ... 'H'm'.

But Sheila was still very much Sheila – bright-eyed, languidly witty and for me always a joy to be with – a joyous person. We talked of our friends; of the May Week Ball (my only one) where Sheila had been my girl; of my desperation when I blurted out 'I ought to rape you now. I really ought.' And Sheila, with a kindly and patient smile: 'But I'd be no good then, would I?' Nothing ever put Sheila out of countenance.

And yet, what struck me most forcibly about coming home after two whole years away, two years out of the world I'd known, was that I'd never really known it – my family in particular. They seemed to have changed so much, developed, grown away from me, that now I was a complete outsider, from another world, another existence. And they? Why, they were going great guns in all sorts of splendid directions.

Suddenly I felt free and hopeful again. What was I doing mooning about here at home when the great new life I'd planned for myself had only just begun? I packed my sea bag, filled my suitcase with all the same kinds of nonsense it always had and always would contain, lashed my oilskins and seaboots on top, then down to the old District Line which had first carried me into the Dagenham marshes two years before. But this time I left it in the city and found my way to Clarkson's shipping office.

Part III
Deep Water Duel

11.

Going Clear

Olivebank was a 4-masted barque and a good deal larger than 3-masted *Killoran* – 2795 compared with 1817 Gross Registered Tons. I found her in Millwall Dock discharging her grain cargo, and went straight aboard.

I felt immediately at home; tossing my gear into a free lower bunk in the forward deckhouse, hauling on dungarees, working shoes, cap; then out on deck and aft to see what the Mate wanted me to start on. A few minutes later I was over the side on a staging, with a chipping hammer in my hand, saying 'Hej!' to Axel West – a chirpy lad from Vasa – and banging away with a will.

What a relief to belong again, to know what was expected of me and how to set about it ... under my own name too; I'd signed on as Seligman, but stuck to Sam as my first name.

On the quayside an artist was at work on a picture of the ship. Axel and I went down in the coffee break to peer over his shoulder.

'What you make?' asked Axel after a bit. I recognised this as an introduction – quite a usual one – rather than an enquiry.

But the artist didn't. 'What d'you think I'm making? Grand Central Station in pastry?'

'Where is Sam and me knacka rost?' persisted Axel.

'Oh, sorry,' said Norman Janes (he later became President of the Marine Artists' Society), and with half a dozen quick strokes – I swear there were only six – he put us both into the picture on our staging.

I still have that picture. He sent it to my father a few weeks later. And I still can't understand how he got us so exactly right with six little brush strokes – Axel lounging, me hammering, and above us a towering edifice of masts and spars and standing rigging, that makes us look small and insignificant.

We sailed about mid-September. We were a happy crowd. But the most important figure in the ship for all of us (and surprisingly, it is isn't always so) was the captain, John Mattson. He was an Ålander, as were all Erikson's captains at that time; and he was a quiet man, who took great care, great pains with everything he did. He never rushed, nor panicked, and he never, never showed off. That was the key to his personality; his judgments were never clouded by vanity. And this, more than anything else, contributed to later triumphs over our great rival, the flagship *Herzogin Cecilie*.

His influence on the ship and her people began to be felt as soon as we slipped the tug. With the wind on his port quarter and the ebb tide under him, another man might have crowded on sail and made a dash for it, straight down Channel. But not Mattson. He seemed to know by instinct when the shift would come. Off Dungeness, with *Olivebank* creaming along at twelve knots under all plain sail, the order came to furl the royals. The sky was clear astern, but ahead high Cirrus streamed eastwards in V-formation, pointing west. Mattson stood by the poop rail on the port side, gazing fixedly to seaward, gauging the run of the swell. Then: 'Steer south-west,' he said to the Second Mate and went below.

That was the start of it. The wind grew stronger as the day wore on and began to veer. By evening we were off the mouth of the Seine, close-hauled on the port tack and heading west. And all through that night the wind contin-ued to veer and freshen, till morning found us off Weymouth Bay and it was time to go about. If we'd

steered a more westerly course from Dungeness, we'd
scarcely have weathered St Catherine's Point.

By the time we got over to the Cherbourg Peninsula on
the starboard tack, it was blowing half a gale and the
upper to'gallants had to come in. Then we went about
again, and by evening we were abreast of Lyme Bay
under topsails and foresail. We had made good progress
and gained a bit of sea room. But now it was blowing a
full gale from west-south-west, and we could see a black
squall building up over Start Point.

All hands were called to get the foresail in and wear ship.
The squall hit us as we battled with the sail. There were ten
of us, including the Third Mate, on the weather yard arm,
fighting a great bag of wind and malice. Although I was in
the port watch, I kept close to Lars Paersch, of the starboard
watch (a lättmatrås, as I was now) who'd already made one
voyage to Australia in *Olivebank*, and knew her well –
where everything was, the weak points here and there (a
block that needed watching, a seizing which ought to be
replaced, and so on) and the feel of her in a seaway. Apart
from this, there was an inner strength in the man that gave
one confidence.

Lars (we called him Lasse) came from a well-to-do
family which, like mine, had mixed origins. But his was
part Swedish, part Finnish, with some German and Russian
blood as well. He was immensely strong: long sinewy arms
and powerful hands to grip and hold the pounding canvas;
long legs to brace firmly against the footrope. He too was
a quiet man, and like me he'd come to sea after a year or
two at University. So there was an immediate bond
between us.

On the next board south we made the Casquets, where
ebbing tidal streams running strongly westwards down Channel, and north-west out of the Bay of St Malo, joined forces
against the wind to kick up mountainous cross seas. *Olivebank*
plunged and rolled and floundered, adding new dimensions to

the work aloft. One had to brace oneself in two directions to get a grip on the sail, then hang on mightily.

As children we had passed this way every summer, and sometimes in the spring as well, on our way to St Jacut-de-la-Mer and its ring of islands, where we first learned to sail. I remembered those shocking cross seas off the Casquets. Then the islands of St Jacut and old Skipper Paitry with his big head and laughing eyes, and Jean Bourseul, his mate. '*Toujours veilleur, jamais peureux,*' they used to tell us. The words, even in memory, had a fortifying ring – up there on the bucking topsail yard. It was reassuring too to look down and see John Mattson standing square and solid on his poop – legs well apart, hands in the side pockets of an old leather jacket; steady, watchful, calm – always calm.

We came about and stood North-West. Already the sky seemed to be lightening in that quarter, but still the shift didn't come – until all at once, way out in mid-Channel, John Mattson turned to the Mate (I was at the wheel at the time) 'Put her round' he said in Swedish 'She'll go clear now'.

I have never been able to discover how he knew. Was it the *smell* of the wind they sometimes talk of, or the run of the swell or just pure magic. I never found out; but round we came, and sure enough, by the time we were up to the wind on the starboard tack, we were heading west-south-west – well to windward of Ushant and all its outlying dangers.

By dawn we were steering south by west, with the wind on our starboard quarter, and bowling along under a press of sail at a good 12 knots or more. The sun burst up into a brilliant sky. The sea sparkled. Coffee pots bubbled on the galley stove. The voyage had begun and we were away.

12.

Sea Meetings

Yes, the voyage had begun well, and it continued in the same way, with only a day or two of flukey winds and calms east of the Azores. Then the North East Trades took us peacefully and comfortably down almost to the equator. That is how I remember it. And the only event during those early days that still remains with me, was the great battle between the carpenter and the heart of a fifteen-foot shark.

Put like that, the incident may sound over-dramatised. But in truth it was a powerful performance. Our carpenter or timmerman (we called him Timpa) had the body of a weight-lifter – short in stature but appallingly muscular. I say 'appallingly' because, when he really chose to exert himself, as he did on this occasion, it could be frightening. And somehow his great round pan of a face with rosy cheeks and curly brown hair – always grinning or chuckling – made it all the more sinister.

We had reached the Doldrums and were lying becalmed. It was a Saturday afternoon and so, as always at such times, a baited shark hook on a chain trace was dangling over the side. There were several sharks about, and we soon had two or three small ones on deck. Then a big one made a lazy grab at the bait and was hauled aboard thrashing and grunting (Plate 7). Or was it roaring – that deep and powerful note which only a furious shark can make?

It was a monster – about fifteen feet long and blue. The boys attacked it with capstan bars, sledge hammers, axes – whatever they could get hold of – as it crashed and thundered around the deck. When it was finally clubbed to death (or so they thought) its fins were cut off to make soup, its tail to be nailed to our bowsprit-end for good luck. Then the stomach was opened in case there might be something interesting inside. And finally the heart was cut out. *It was still beating.*

For some reason this infuriated Timpa. He rushed off to his shop and brought back a ten pound flogging hammer, with which he struck the heart a great blow. It bounced. He struck it again. It bounced and bounced ...*and went on beating.*

Timpa kept on smashing at that heart. Then in a rage he gripped it in one of his massive hands and squeezed. This was the moment of truth, we thought. His eyes blazed and seemed almost to start from his head, a little froth of saliva formed in one corner of his mouth with the tremendous force he put into that terrible squeeze. The effect was frightening. For a moment or two nothing happened. Then, very slowly, his fingers were being forced apart, and the heart came bulging between them. And those bulges of greyish-red flesh were *beating rhythmically in unison.*

Timpa gave up then. And after a while the various bits and entrails were thrown overboard, and the carcass after them. Then the watch below went to dinner and forgot about sharks, until suddenly someone on deck shouted. We all tumbled out and rushed to the ship's side. There was the disembowelled, finless and tailless body of the shark *swimming* slowly, very slowly past.

The ship was still dead becalmed. The shark swam all the way round her, the tail end of its body (without a tail) waving languidly from side to side. Its progress was barely perceptible, and yet, after fifteen minutes or so, it had reached the bow and was turning slowly round it. Then down the starboard side, keeping the same distance from the ship's hull – about ten feet – all the way round. Whether it could see or not I don't know, or even whether live sharks can see; perhaps they maintain direction by some sort of sonar – a nervous reaction to light and dark, or hard and soft, or just by smell. At all events this one kept close to the ship, and after nearly an hour came back up the portside to where its own guts were floating in the water.

It nosed in amongst them and then, very lethargically, began to feed. I still have a vivid mental picture of that shark's jaws just open and a ribbon of entrail trailing out on one side. It was an eerie sight.

What would have happened next is difficult to imagine. The shark had no stomach. In fact its own stomach was one of the tit-bits it was trying to swallow. Anyway, just then a puff of wind came along and we were called to the braces. When we got back, the shark and its strange feast had disappeared astern.

We caught no more sharks that trip. The puff of breeze that found us was from the east, and slowly it gained in strength till by sunset we were steering 'full-and-by' to the first of the South-East Trades. And for the next two weeks we went thundering southwards with sheets eased and the warm wind singing aloft. Those were indeed the halcyon days – at the wheel, in the rigging or on look-out at night – with the wind washing over you, round you and through your hair, warm and caressing or cool and invigorating according to your mood.

There were twenty-eight of us on board, but only a few come into this story, notably two – Berglund, the sailmaker, and Koskinen – who were always rubbing up against each other, striking sparks and generating heat in the age-old discord between mainland Finns and Swedish Finns from Åland, which coloured the lives of all on board, even those who belonged to neither faction.

Berglund was a typical Swede – blonde, well-built and capable; about six feet tall, with a bland Scandinavian type of face and flaxen hair. He had a fine strong body, broad shoulders, narrow hips, sturdy legs, and took his position as senior petty officer very seriously. He could be reserved to the point of rudeness, but he was kindly and cheerful at heart. Most people liked him and all looked up to him.

Except Koskinen, the Finn. He was a horse of another colour altogether. 'Spectacular' is the word that describes him best: six feet three in his socks (when he wore any), muscles like a prize-fighter and strikingly handsome in a laughing, dark-skinned Spanish sort of way. Aristocratic too, with his long straight nose, black hair and dark flashing eyes. Some said he'd been an officer in the Finnish navy, but there was trouble. Maybe he socked his Admiral – if he happened to be an Ålander.

Ashore in his lightweight check suit, trousers always immaculately pressed (under his mattress), hair parted in the middle and heavily oiled, broad-brimmed biscuit-coloured hat in hand, a scarlet handkerchief lolling from his breast pocket, brown and white co-respondents' shoes and a big cigar in his teeth, you'd have taken Koskinen for an Argentinian millionaire at least, or even a top flight film star. But he was pure Finn, through and through.

He was always laughing and gentle with the younger ones – when he was sober. That was his only real defect, but it was very real. When drunk he could be a terror. All his Finnish fighting spirit would come to the top and set him roaring. When you saw him stepping languidly down the gangway (he always went ashore alone), you'd pray that he wouldn't get half drunk, fighting drunk – that he'd get blind drunk or find a good strong woman to keep him occupied all night and send him back sober in the morning.

Yet at sea, Koskinen was incomparable, with more than his share of that quality the Finns call 'Sisu', a combination of courage, ferocity, strength and sheer determination, which enables them to triumph, in war and peace, against stupendous odds. Koskinen would stand at the braces with big seas boarding, long after everyone else had leaped for the lifelines – howling defiance at the sea and insults at his shipmates, till the next wave smothered him in an avalanche of green water. And even then he'd never let go.

Then there was Walter Hoffman, a young apprentice, from Lüneburg, in northern Germany. I nearly forgot him; he was such a shy, retiring short of chap. When you first met him you wondered how such a sensitive youngster came to choose the life at sea. And yet young Walter had already, at the age of sixteen, been through a more testing sea experience than any of us on board – a full dismasting in a hurricane-force squall, with him aloft when the masts came crashing down.

Hoffman had joined us in what was almost a pierhead jump. The tug brought him off at Gravesend when she came alongside to put her hawser aboard. He hadn't even time to stow his gear, which was dumped on the main hatch while he tailed on with the others to secure the hawser and cat the anchor.

No one took much notice of him. The other two apprentices, both German and both older, greeted him briefly, but as a new boy: they'd been in the ship a few weeks themselves. And it was several days before we found out that he'd already made one voyage to Australia in the 4-masted barque *Hougomount*.

We knew about her, of course. She'd been dismasted on the voyage out, in April, and finally limped into Adelaide under jury rig about mid-May. It was now September, so Hoffman must have come straight home and off again to sea in *Olivebank* – a ship of the same size and type, bound on exactly the same voyage. And when he eventually told us about that desperate night we marvelled.

At midnight on April 20th, with a freshening westerly wind, four of them had been sent aloft to furl the fore upper to'gallant, which had burst from its gear and was thrashing wild. Suddenly, without any warning, a black cloud came racing up astern, bringing with it a squall of terrific violence. The upper to'gallant yard buckled and broke, hurling them into the rigging, as the masts – all four of them – came down in a splintering tangle of ropes, spars and canvas.

How they all escaped was a mystery – flung this way and that, with blocks and wires flailing round them in the darkness and the crests of big seas sweeping the decks. Yet none of them was seriously hurt. And here was young Hoffman, smiling his shy, sensitive smile, setting out cool as a cucumber on another long, stormy voyage in sail.

And so into the Westerlies once again; with eight thousand miles of easting to Australia still before us. Spring was well advanced and the weather fair. We picked up the West winds in latitude 32°S and stood east-by-south for the Cape.

It was on this voyage that Lasse and I first saw Tristan da Cunha, rising dark and forbidding out of the sea on the southern horizon. A drift of white cloud (it may have been steam) hung wavering but never dissolving from the top of its 7000ft peak. For a long time we watched but nothing stirred, no flicker of life.

'It must be the loneliest place one earth,' said someone.

'And yet folk live there. More than a hundred, I've been told.'

'I wonder what they do.'

'One day', said Lasse, 'we'll land there and find out.' I remember neither calms nor storms nor head-winds on this part of the voyage, until just south of the Cape itself, when one of the south-easterly gales, for which those waters are notorious, piped up out of a clear sky. It increased steadily throughout the afternoon – a dead head wind for *Olivebank*. So at nightfall John Mattson decided to put her head under her wing, as they say: he shortened right down to lower topsails and main upper topsail; no foresail even. And there we lay all night, virtually hove-to on the starboard tack, nudging gently eastwards into a rising sea.

But fairly comfortable, and nothing to worry about, until

just as day was breaking there came a cry of 'Sail Ho!' and we saw the tall grey column of a square-rigger under to'gallants and royals, bearing down on us out of the mist on the port quarter.

It was *Herzogin Cecilie*, a 4-masted barque like ourselves, but built more recently and in a very different style. Where *Olivebank*, launched on the Clyde in 1892, had a graceful sheer and low freeboard, *Herzogin* built ten years later as a training ship for the famous Norddeutscher Lloyd Company of Hamburg, was a more powerful vessel altogether, with high sides and heavy rigging. She was the flagship of the Erikson fleet, and her skipper, Sven Erikson, was a young man with a great reputation for hard driving in all weathers. She tore past us, heeled right over under her press of canvas. She must have been doing all of 15 knots, and she soon disappeared into the haze and wrack on the northern horizon.

John Mattson watched her in silence. I can see him now, with his steady, calm gaze and the faintest smile on his lips. We waited for the order to make sail and go after her, but it never came. And all that day, and through the night, we jogged steadily on, steering with care, to keep her clean full and moving. We made all the easting we could without any fuss, and at midnight we wore ship onto the port tack, but that was all.

By dawn the gale had increased. We edged along into it, calm and steady, when all at once there was *Herzogin* again, looming out of the northern haze; with her royals furled now, but still carrying upper to'gallants on all three of her square-rigged masts. She was close-hauled on the port tack and heeled right over by the force of the wind; tearing along in clouds of spray at a good 12 knots or more, *but still astern of us*. With all his dashing about and crowding on sail, Sven Erikson hadn't gained a metre on John Mattson – not a metre – and soon he'd disappeared again into mist to the south of us.

Next day the wind came fair and sent us bowling eastward in fine style (Plate 8). In the first five days we covered 1,850 sea miles. In one period of 24 hours we logged 380 miles, and for the whole of one watch we averaged 17 knots. This was great sailing. No one had ever tried to make *Olivebank* do her best before – given her a chance to show her paces. John Mattson took no risks, but he watched her day and night and kept her sailing at her own best speed. He seemed to have a deep and inner understanding of her. If ever a captain was at one with his ship, he certainly was.

We made a passage of 22 days from the Cape to Australia, and as each splendid day followed day, we soon forgot about *Herzogin Cecilie*. We never expected to see her again. Such meetings are rare, and if she was getting the same weather as we, she'd most likely be ahead of us by now, we thought, if that was what Sven Erikson had in mind. So we forgot her – right up until the afternoon we raised Kangaroo Island, in the mouth of the Spencer Gulf of South Australia, when for the third time that voyage it was 'Sail Ho!' And there she was yet again, *and still astern of us*.

The wind was dead fair, and we were running with squared yards. Sven Erikson tried every trick in the book to overtake us – even 'tacking down wind' – that is, bringing the wind first on one quarter, then on the other, so that all the sails on all three square-rigged masts were kept full and drawing. But it was no use. John Mattson, that calm and careful man, watched him with the ghost of a friendly smile, as we stood steadily on into the Spencer Gulf, while he finally bore away for Adelaide. And he never caught us!

13.

Cross Purposes

Port Lincoln is a natural harbour, in a hook of land on the western side of the entrance to Spencer Gulf. From a hill behind the town you can look out over the open ocean, six or seven miles away, yet the harbour itself is completely enclosed, with Boston Island across the entrance to shelter it from the east.

The town looked inviting as we sailed into the bay, with red-roofed houses among trees and a jetty thronged with people out for their evening stroll. We longed to join them on what clearly took the place of the squares and promenades of European cities. But we'd called only for orders, so the Captain went ashore alone in the agents' launch, returning late without any definite news.

That night we shifted on the land breeze to the outer anchorage and next morning started to discharge some of our 1600 tons of ballast. This was where donkeyman Vuori became the man of the moment and we his slaves. He fired his boiler with timber and coal till it juddered and blew off continuously, while we sweated down the hold filling great baskets with rocks, stones and rubble. These were whipped out and over the side on two falls; one rove through a gin-block on a span between the fore and main rigging, the other through another gin on the fore yard arm. 'Donkey' was the complete controller and master of ceremonies: it was his hour and he made the most of it. The mates left him to it.

After the Captain, Ragnar Vuori was the most important

man in the ship and remarkable in many ways. First and foremost he was a clown. Both his face and body had the appearance and texture of India rubber. So had his mind. It was a bouncing, chuckling sort of mind, full of Rabelaisian humour and a tremendous bonhomie. Though he was the most experienced petty officer on board and a prime seaman (he had sailed in Yankee schooners, and steamers too), he preferred the social life of the forecastle to that of the petty officers' cabin or the apprentices' half-deck.

He bounded about, he roared, he laughed. He had no side and was never patronising, even to the youngest 'jungman'. He told impossible stories ... 'Was I keen? Was I? Oh boy, I tell you I went after her up Broadway on my knees at a rate of knots, and you couldn't see the lights in Times Square for the blue flames shooting out of me arse.' And he'd do a little dance in his excitement, his broad flat feet slapping the wooden deck like penguin's flippers.

But now, with the ballast to shift, Vuori was seaman first and all the time. There followed three days of blazing heat and dust and ill humour, during which the watches were only allowed ashore for two or three hours each on successive evenings.

Our orders came through at last. We were to load at Port Victoria, on the other side of the Gulf. This was bad news. A ship of our size couldn't get alongside at Port Vic. We'd have to lie half a mile or more off-shore and load from auxiliary ketches, who would bring the bags out to us, about 500 at a time, with three or four lumpers to handle them. It might take months – six or seven weeks anyway – with shore leave restricted and difficult to organise.

When we reached the Port Vic roadstead, we found two other sailing vessels already there and loading – *Mozart*, an Erikson four-masted barquentine, and *Priwal*, a 5000-ton German 'P' Line training ship, built in the 1920s to make

hard-fought passages eastwards round Cape Horn to Val-
paraiso and back with nitrates. The white ketches, motoring
busily between them and the jetty, took no notice of
Olivebank till well on into the following afternoon. We
were clearly in for a long, hot spell in harbour.

I don't remember the name of the pub; it was the one we
always went to. I was sitting at the end of the bar near the
window, waiting for Jim Corven, one of the lumpers, and his
wife to pick me up. It was a scorching afternoon. The glare
from the white dust of the roadway, and white-fronted houses
with corrugated iron roofs painted dark red, was overpowering.
It pierced one's eyes like hot needles, deadening the brain.

A few of our lads came in and sat down at a table in
the corner. There was Berglund, the sailmaker, Timpa,
Axel West, Sandholm and one or two others. Sandholm
had his fiddle with him; he was a Swedish Finn from the
mainland, and he too, it was rumoured, had once been a
naval officer. He was a quiet and rather unassuming
fellow, who used, I think, to play his violin to help him
control a craving for hard liquor. They were the few who
had no special friends ashore, so they were having a
Saturday afternoon pub crawl on their own. Axel raised a
hand and smiled at me. The rest took no notice. Sandholm
began to play softly to himself.

Presently Koskinen came in. One could see at once that
he was well on in drink. Most probably he'd been out in the
bush on his own with a bottle of whisky, a favourite trick of
his. He was not gregarious by nature; there was indeed a
strange, almost mystical streak in him – half Nordic, half
Magyar – which sometimes set him brooding and apart. In
earlier days he would have been known as a warlock Finn,
and perhaps that was what he felt himself to be.

He stood swaying in the doorway, staring fixedly (as
fixedly as he was able) at the party in the corner. They
took no notice, but they were aware of him. One could

tell by the sailmaker's rather forced smile as he leant forward to drink an entirely unnecessary toast with Timpa; by the way Axel West giggled; by the simultaneous decision of two jungmän, who weren't special friends, to buy each other another drink, and the futile little argument that followed.

'Satan's Ålänningar,' muttered Koskinen, and slouched up to the bar. Then loudly 'Drink! ... for all, drink! ... for all who is here, visky!' Then he glanced balefully round at the two jungmän who, being further perplexed by this sudden interruption, abandoned their polite little argument and sat down. They stared, smiling uncertainly, first at Koskinen then at the sailmaker, who now rose, meandered deliberately up to the bar, and said 'Rom' in a loud voice.

Koskinen spread his legs, tipped his broad-brimmed hat onto the back of his head and glared at Berglund. The sweat was pouring down his face 'I ask visky' he roared, rocking back on his heels, then recovering. 'All vill drink visky! Satan's Ålänningar!'

Berglund swung round, eyes blazing. 'Hold your mouth! You hear?' Then, turning away, 'Finn Hellscum!'

Koskinen hauled off to aim a mighty blow. But, to everyone's surprise, the fight was stopped before it started by the cheerful little Aussie barman, who butted in stridently with ...'No go. Beer or nothin' for the lot o' youse.'

Both turned and glared at the barman, forgetting their country's eternal race problem.

'You not have visky?'

'Or Rom?'

'Not fer youse jokers, I ain't.'

'For hell!' shouted Koskinen. 'I strook you down!'

'Aw, why can't you bastards 'ave a dance, or somethin'? You couldn't stroke a kitty-cat with measles, the way you are!' The little Aussie grinned at them both disarmingly.

Koskinen hesitated a moment, still glaring, then slouched

to the door. There he swung round and suddenly began yelling at the top of his voice, '*Olivebank* Finnish ship. I am Finn. Here is only Satan's Swedes and foreigners. *Olivebank* Finnish ship. My ship. Satan an Satan an Perkele!' And he'd gone, zig-zagging down the street.

'Poetical bastard, ain't 'e?' observed the barman pleasantly. Berglund sat down.

Through the small window beside me I watched Koskinen lurching down the wide road, kicking up white dust at every step. A dog rushed at him barking. He aimed a kick at it that sent him staggering and lurching, till he fetched up lolling against the wall of the Bank. He heaved himself up and staggered on between the two rows of shacks and bungalows with their small dried-up patches of garden.

Fences, over which the bougainvillea straggled forlornly, separated each plot from the roadway and from its neighbour. There was no colour except the rusty red of the roofs and the faded purple of bougainvillea, stretching their parched necks down towards the footpath, like snakes in search of water. And there *was* no water in all that dust and heat and glare under a white hot sky.

Weaving from side to side, with every now and then a little staggering run, this way or that, to regain his balance, Koskinen struggled on down the street and out into the bush – growing smaller with distance and less important – like a bewildered beetle plodding uncertainly towards the scrubbery of thorn and bush and cactus whence it had come.

14.

Sunday

The job of nightwatchman in a ship at anchor in calm weather is a pleasant one: no gangway to watch for stray drunks, no moorings to tend; a time for thought, for plans and counter-plans.

The night wears on, continuing calm. Time drags interminably. And how still it is; not a breath to stir the surface of the sea, or sound in the rigging. Aft, beyond the galley with its lighted doorway, the deck lies drowned in shadow. Out of it the masts emerge like giant banyans spangled with stars and garmented with ropes which fall like aerial roots about them.

It is still quite dark when the flood begins to make, and a breath of wind comes sauntering off the land. *Olivebank* stirs to life. A low-voiced argument begins between blocks and parrals, as the yards strain against their braces – like the mutter of people turning in their sleep. It dies away soon, but this sudden stirring has broken in upon my thoughts. The false dawn has passed already: the true dawn is at hand. Stars begin to pale, then fly away upwards, becoming pinpoints first, then vanishing altogether.

The door of Vuori's cabin amidships flies open and slams back against the steel side of the deckhouse. The cat springs delicately onto the storm step and pours itself down into the greying shadows outside. Vuori's heavily tattooed brown arm reaches out and pulls the door to again.

This is reveille. After hauling down the riding light on the fore stay, I go aft for the handle of the fresh water pump to begin the day's routine.

The waking of a ship to life on a Sunday is a different affair from the surly shake she gives herself on weekdays. On a working day there is no sleepy stretch and then a smile on opening her eyes; she is caught and set upon, while still half-dreaming, by the turmoil of commercial life – a life that keeps innumerable jumps ahead of her throughout the day – rough, heavy-booted jumps that make her shudder. But on Sundays ... in the first place there are eggs for breakfast, and time to enjoy them.

Lilla Lotta

When I take the coffee forward, the sun is already streaming in at the starboard door and portholes of the forecastle. It shines engagingly through the many-coloured bunk curtains, and sends a slanting shaft across the belly of Lilla Lotta, or Spirit of the North, as she is also sometimes called.

We are very proud of Lilla Lotta who occupies the centre of the forward bulkhead. Each voyage, when the forecastle is painted out, the best artist on board is deputed to freshen her up. Under the brushes of successive admirers her breasts have swollen and grown grotesquely long, her belly bloated and her hips broadened out of all proportion – out of proportion, that is, with her head, which no-one ever bothers to repaint.

This crudely impressionistic figure lies, with the Flag of Finland waving over her, on a tangle of branches, fir-cones, pine needles and the like which, judging by her agonised grin and indecorously angled legs, cause her considerable discomfort.

Cabin Boys

The half-deck aft, under the standard compass, is divided into two separate cabins. In the large, forward cabin live the German apprentices – Horst Scheibel, a Silesian; Adrian Leimbach, from Heidelberg; and Walter Hoffman. The after cabin is shared by the carpenter and the sailmaker (who is also the bosun, by the way). The cook and steward share a cabin in the poop.

The steward is a mysterious fellow, with a long hound-like face and three prominent gold teeth in a little cluster on one side of his mouth. He has been with the company for several years. He is a silent man, though by no means taciturn; it is simply that he speaks Swedish with difficulty and has never learned English.

Master

Captain Mattson is already on the poop when I go aft to make five bells. He is always out on the stroke of half-past six on a Sunday morning, pacing up and down in his pyjamas, scratching his bottom and breaking wind luxuriously from time to time. The sound and sight of his brightly-coloured sleeping suit is as much a part of Sunday morning as the special Sunday ensign which I shall presently fetch from the Mate's cabin and hoist on the ensign-staff.

John Mattson is moderately tall, thick set and has a friendly, unemotional sort of face – a face that gives confidence without inspiring awe. His greenish eyes will look at you directly, but they are seldom hard or angry. They are accustomed eyes, accustomed to examining the hearts of men and the weight of an approaching squall with equal understanding.

I lift my cap and say good morning, to which he replies with a nod and a smile. Then I go aft and make six bells on the small bell on the steering-gear casing. In due course, the hands are mustered on the quarter deck, and some of them come up the poop ladder with cleaning gear in their hands, to start on the bright work.

The hour before breakfast on a Sunday is one of the pleasantest of the week. First up the poop ladder (a habit of theirs) come the German apprentices: Scheibel followed by Leimbach and Hoffman, in that order – in that invariable order. They are a strange trio, forever going into earnest conclave (summoned by Scheibel) about some special action they propose to take. Wearing their uniform caps for polishing brass on Sundays is one of these. They do it so that they can give a proper salute to the Captain. He acknowledges their greetings with a friendly wave and a tolerant smile.

Discipline, what there is of it on a Sunday, is largely self-imposed. We confer on easy terms with the mates about small details – coiling down ropes in a specially decorative manner, for instance, or ... 'A dab of gold paint on the truck of the ensign staff, third Mate?'

'Bra. And de treads on de poop ladders, ve polish dem dis morning.'

Stern Teutonic voice from the background ... 'And show these Aussies what we call a smart ship, eh?'

'No. Because it look good, för Satan.' Even the third Mate, easy-going and a friend to all, finds Horst Scheibel a bit much at times. But on the whole, and despite rumours of impending war, we like the apprentices. They are *our* apprentices, our shipmates – a stronger bond in all our minds than any nationalism, even theirs.

Adrian Leimbach, in particular, is a fine type of Nordic giant (Plate 9). He's good-natured too, and intelligent. In consequence, he has a sense of humour which must, one would have thought, cause him some uneasiness when they are making their little National Socialist demonstrations.

It doesn't though. If anything, it enables him to play his part in a a more relaxed and confident manner than the others. 'For a German to salute his captain,' he explains (in faultless English with a cultured accent) 'is no more unreasonable than to make use of the appropriate convenience for the natural functions of the body. Neither will prolong one's life appreciably, but both, if neglected, are apt to involve one in tiresome explanations.' An English sentence, to Leimbach, is like a glass of good wine. He likes to feel it rolling round his tongue, and always tries to make it last as long as possible.

Horst Scheibel is tall and thin, with a straight-lipped, passionless sort of face. And although he never behaves with undue arrogance – except to his messmates in the half-deck – one can see that he's determined at all times to control his environment. Meanwhile, under the current craze for National Socialism he is a bit unsure of himself; Leimbach and Hoffman too, though it causes them less concern. Being young and frequently away at sea, they can never be quite sure of how they ought to react – would be expected to react – to the unbridled ways and loose practices of the decadent democrats who surround them. So to be on the safe side, all three click their heels on Sunday mornings and salute. Their short-clipped 'Herr Kapitän' ... 'tag Herr Kapitän' ... 'Kapitän' ... ring out upon the Sabbath air in quick succession, slick as music hall patter (which in many ways they resemble) ... to everyone's amusement, including the Captain's.

John Mattson knows they are trying to militarise him, make him assume what they consider to be the correct bearing for an officer on duty; possibly even force him to wear some kind of uniform himself, a thing he would never dream of doing before breakfast on a Sunday. So, unabashed, he strolls at his ease pyjama-ed on the poop, offering his gaudy flanks to the slanting sunlight, and to the breeze an amiably trumpeting behind.

After all, *Olivebank* is an Åland ship, which means that the captain, all the officers and some of the men come from the same kind of homes – small wooden houses dotted about among the pine forests and islands of their native archipelago. Their families have been neighbours for centuries. Many of them are related, and all come from a race of traditional landowners – independent landowners. Even the poorest and simplest of them are natural aristocrats, by ancestry as well as by upbringing.

And they are polite, these islanders, having no incentive to be otherwise in the classless communities of fishermen-farmers from which they come. So they lift their caps and say 'Gu' moron', with ease and sincerity. And the captain answers: 'Gu' moron'.

15.

Fair Wind to Cape Horn

Dawn was just stealing over the land to windward as we slipped the tug *Nelsebee's* hawser. She gave us the customary farewell toots on her whistle and fell astern. As the sun burst up over the hills, it shone on our sails, turning us instantly into a castle of gold. The ship forged ahead over the sheltered waters of the Gulf; stepping out from her dusty seven-week bondage with a fresh beam wind out of a clear and brilliant sky.

Our setting out on the voyage home had been so sudden and unexpected that even now, though we were clear of Hardwicke Bay and standing south-by-west down the Gulf, it was difficult to realise that we were actually at sea. There'd been a Grand Dance the evening before and half the crew had gone ashore to it. When they came aboard again, about 2.00 a.m., the rest of us were roused at once. Then the *Nelsebee* secured alongside and we were away.

By 10.00 a.m. we had Cape Spencer abeam to port, with the Neptune Islands broad to starboard. But at noon the wind fell light, and by four bells we lay becalmed about fifteen miles north of Cape Borda on the Western end of Kangaroo Island.

As the sky remained clear, it quickly grew very hot on deck. But about six in the evening a breeze came to us off the land, and in less than a minute the ship had gathered way again. The wind freshened, the ship lay over. Water spouted up through the scupper holes and set the wash-ports clanging. Before it grew dark we had left the land astern and were thrusting southwards at 9-10 knots to clear the western coast of Tasmania.

Saturday, February 4

While we were in port all the topsail sheets and some others were renewed, and several new whips rove into the braces. We also have a new suit of sails, and extra staysails are being hanked on to the main and mizzen to'gallant stays.

Apparently some of the skippers met one evening in Adelaide last week. There was some powerful drinking and a good deal of boasting. *Herzogin Cecilie, Penang, Favell, Archibald Russell* and *Abraham Rydberg* all sailed a few days before we did, and some of the others aren't far behind. So there may be a real race between us all this year.

South of New Zealand, in Latitude 50°S, it began to blow. That was on February 10th, and for the next five days all hands were needed continuously, so that it was difficult to remember which watch ought in any case to be on deck and which below. Either there were sails or the remnants of sails to battle with aloft, or replacements to bend on, or braces to be hauled (watching your chance between big seas boarding). At times so much water was thundering about the decks that it was safer and more practical to keep all hands aft on the poop – some nominally on watch, some dozing (either standing against the rigging with an arm crooked round the gear, or lolling on deck with a rope's end round you, in case a sea came over, even up there, and washed you about).

Olivebank ran and ran before a whole gale from the west (Plate 10), backing later to south-west and freezing cold. At night it was bitter. The Southern Cross hanging well up in the sky and Antares glowing orange in the Scorpion's head seemed to stare at us fiercely until the dawn refined them into glittering jewels, then pin points before they disappeared.

On the third day the wind came round to west-north-west with rain and sleet. Gunnar Sandblom, able seaman, a stout-hearted, cheerful lad from Hangö had a No.2 Box Brownie camera. He wanted to get a picture that really captured the spirt of that blow. With his camera on the poop rail, set at one twenty-fifth of a second, and Lasse and I on either side, propping him up against the roll of the ship, he waited for the precise moment to shoot (Plate 11).

About once a day the cook would try to get forward along the lifeline to his galley and drop in through the skylight. He was quite a guy, that cook. He'd light his fire, and he might be lucky; then again he might not, a big sea might come crashing in and put it out. The skylight was smashed and had to be boarded up; and twice, trying to get some hot food back aft in a bucket he was washed away down the deck, bucket and all.

On Monday, March 6th we sighted the peaks of Diego Ramirez and passed them in moonlight that evening. Thirty-four days to the Horn was good going, and everyone was in the best of spirits. We wondered how the other ships were faring, and less than 12 hours later we found out. At dawn on March 7th, there was *Herzogin* right ahead. And we were coming up on her fast! Soon we were abreast.

With a stiff northerly breeze blowing clouds of spray off the tops of rising seas, she bore away then and came down to us. It was a magnificent sight. The sun was shining through a light haze. She plunged and reared in the short, steep seas. They piled under her bowsprit and leaped smoking over the weather rail of her foredeck. Her bows came down, turning the green water aside into gleaming hills and a smother of foam.

We furled the fore and mizzen royals; then brailed in the head of the spanker and hauled down the gaff topsail. This allowed her to come right up under our stern, half a cable away, so that the two Captains could shout to each other through speaking trumpets. The thunder of her bow wave was louder than the sound of the seas passing down our sides. A man I was shipmates with in *Killoran* stood on her forecastle head; I could recognise him easily.

Next day, March 8th, *Herzogin* was still with us (Plate 13), though we had shortened sail again during the night. John Mattson didn't want to get too far to the eastward; he saw a shift coming, so he held well up to the wind, biding his time. But Sven Erikson, as before off the Cape, crowded on sail and filled away, disappearing soon into haze on the eastern horizon. We heard later that he'd held on eastwards for twenty-four hours, and next day found himself among icebergs.

Meanwhile, there were some 30 degrees of latitude to struggle through before we could expect reliable winds. Horse latitudes! The hard, ferocious westerlies, for which you had braced yourself and been prepared, are behind you. The halcyon days are ahead. And in between? What is there in between, but doubts, uncertainties, and flukey weather, dragging you this way and that? No heart, no body in the wind, nor in the calms between. Horse latitudes! The featureless regions of the sea that bring out the finer, more enduring qualities in ships and men.

One learns, above all, to appreciate simple pleasures. I recall an almost sensual delight in the first real wash after weeks in oilskins from Australia to the Horn. On the first warm Saturday after passing the Falkland Islands and entering the 'horse latitudes', all hands would heat their buckets of fresh water on the galley stove, then strip and scrub themselves all over, before putting on clean under-clothes, clean shirts, dry trousers, socks and slippers.

After that some might patiently pare their broken nails; some would even scent themselves with eau-de-cologne. And as often as not, a final gale would come rollicking after us, sending everyone back into oilskins and seaboots. It didn't matter. That first all-round wash of the passage had been a luxury beyond all luxuries.

Plate 1 … just a box really …

Plate 2 The Doldrums.

Plate 3 George Londén.

Plate 4 ... when big seas come aboard ...

Plate 5 ... all freshwater tanks full ...

Plate 6 *(opposite)* ... thundering southwards ...

Plate 7 … and was hauled aboard …

Plate 8 … bowling eastwards in fine style …

Plate 9 ... a fine type of Nordic giant ...

Plate 10 … ran and ran before a whole gale from the west …

Plate 11 … waited for the precise moment to shoot …

Plate 12 … the focus of all our thoughts …

Plate 13 Next day *Herzogin* was still with us …

Plate 14 … took station on our port quarter …

Plate 15 … sculled the boat into the narrows.

Plate 16 … to build some kind of cabin.

Plate 17 … transporting all the green staff we could find …

Plate 18 … on Saturdays and Sundays we were free …

Plate 19 ... we fought with it for nearly an hour ...

Plate 20 *(opposite)* ... forging powerfully southwards
through glittering seas ...

Plate 21 … sailed alongside under topsails.

It used, I remember, to have a strangely intoxicating effect: sleeping was difficult after it. One became seized instead by a passion for squaring up and bringing out on deck all one's queer belongings – the clothes, the books, the stuffed lizard (gone a bit on one side), the string of shells, half-finished models, letters from Liz, and the patent marlin-spike that never really worked. All would be spread in the sunshine, gloated over, sorted, sighed at, classified I don't know how, then stowed away again to become at once the dear and senseless jumble they had always been – of passing whims, ideas, ambitions, memories – which sometimes give us the feeling that we're really not such duds: just look what we could have been or had or done if we had wanted to – if we had never 'sold that farm to go to sea'.

The winds remained light, variable, unsteady, mainly unfavourable and utterly damnable. But everyone seemed to be in good spirits for all that. We were steadily working our way up into warmer latitudes, and that wave of optimism which began with our 34-day passage to the Horn was carrying us onward still.

Thursday, March 16th
Today the pigs were let out on deck and spent all morning galloping from one end of the ship to the other, eating everything they could find, including any clothing which had been left about.

For two days now we have been beating through soft warm northerly air, and today it was actually hot. Men were going about in lighter clothes. Mattresses were brought out on to the main hatch. In the evening came one of those breath-taking sunset skies, whose colours are too glaring to be artistic – long streaks of fiery orange, bright scarlet, rich crimson against an ochre background, and under that the sea turned stony black by contrast.

Friday, March 24th : Pampero

The gale, when it came, was short but extremely violent. Pamperos, they call them, off the River Plate. There was a sudden spite in it that was terrifying at first.

In particular, I remember an awed hush that fell on the ship as the sun went down and the sky turned from orange to an unhealthy tawny colour. There was something leprous and vilely threatening about that sky. It acted like a filter, cutting out every shade of blue, so that men's faces suddenly glowed an unearthly red – not from reflected light, the sky itself was putty-coloured, but as though a raging scarlet fever had struck the whole company.

We looked at each other and laughed nervously, with a superstitious dread inside us. When we talked, our voices were low; we almost whispered, for fear of giving offence to the advancing storm, whose livid tendrils of cloud were already writhing out towards the ship.

It fell upon us just before midnight. The ship staggered and lay over under a great burden of sail, burying her lee rail again and again until she seemed too weary to rise, and all we saw for a while were the upper ends of her rigging screws tearing through the sea alongside, like soldiers in single file hurrying to keep up with her mad career. Lumps and streamers of brilliant phosphorescence, carried aft by a torrent of warm sea water sweeping down the deck, tore by in the opposite direction.

All hands had been called at once to shorten sail. They came out helter-skelter half-clothed. But the water was warm, and thrashing about in it was fun. We hove and hurried hilariously from rope to rope, laughing and shouting, though the masts were dangerously overburdened and the Captain looked anxious. The upper to'gallants, mainsail and crossjack were furled. The lower to'gallants came next, and it was then that the full force of the storm struck.

Buntlines carried away their lizards. A clew-line parted.

Four of us were sent aloft in the fore rigging to do what we could. The decks, in any case, had become impassable; but it was not until we reached the topmast shrouds that we felt the full weight of the wind. It pinned us to the rigging till we could hardly breathe.

The next two hours were a nightmare. The sail, normally well within the power of two men to stow, had burst from its gear. It was thundering and thrashing away from the yard with the force of a thousand demons. You had to make a continuous effort to cling on. At any moment, you felt, the braces must go and the yard fly out of control ...

Now gradually the wind began to back. The ship, coming up to her course, started to rear and plunge into a high head sea, burying her bows, then lifting to send great surges of water cataracting aft, at times covering the poop itself. We wondered how they fared on deck as we heard first a staysail, then a topsail blow to pieces.

Three times we beat our own sail into temporary submission. Three times it tore loose again with a snarl, parting stout gaskets as though they'd been twine. Then it split, and once again we struggled to windward and strove with it. Buntline wires beat on our backs and legs; other wires, shackles and blocks whistled about our ears or knocked sparks from the yards. But at last, quite suddenly, it was over; someone got hold of the clew and the rest of us threw ourselves on the bunt of the sail.

When we got on deck, we found that two braces and a bowsprit shroud, as well as any amount of lesser gear, had carried away. Then the wind died as suddenly as it had arisen, and by daybreak the watch on deck were already making sail, to take full advantage of a freshening sou-wester, our first fair wind since rounding the Horn.

16.

Race to the Line

Just before dawn on Sunday, March 26th, in Latitude 34° 30'S, with a fresh south-westerly blowing, the carpenter reported a light, way out on the starboard quarter; and when daylight came we could just make out a square-rigged ship about ten miles off abeam. She altered course towards, and we soon saw that it was *Herzogin*. She crossed our stern about two miles off and took station on our port quarter (Plate 14), where she remained all day.

From now on, remote and isolated from the world and its affairs, *Herzogin Cecilie* became once again the focus of all our thoughts (Plate 12) – the very object of our existence. Although the South East Trades – the full fair winds we had relied upon to carry us up the Atlantic – although the Trades failed us, the wind eventually drew eastwards, but blew mainly from a bit north of east. So both ships were close hauled, steering 'full and by'. And sometimes we had to brace sharp up, instead of easing sheets to gain a bit of speed.

On this point of sailing, *Herzogin* could hold us and a bit more; but the moment the wind freed a little, *Olivebank* moved ahead. So for the most part we sailed north-by-east together. Yet it was a race not so much between us and them – both ships were Finnish with mainly Åland crews – but between the ships themselves: one a proud and powerful German, built in Hamburg in 1902, the other a long, lean and extremely graceful lady, reflecting in her lines, in her tall and slender spars, the artistry of her Clydeside designers.

Yes, this race in the solitude and far horizons of the sea, had come to dominate our lives. A man going aft to the galley at sunrise for our coffee, would cast his eyes to leeward as soon as he was clear of the lee fore rigging. If *Herzogin* was there, sailing abreast of us, he'd pause for a moment to watch her standing stolidly northwards, noting the set of her sails, how her jibs were drawing, how her upper yards were braced, and try to gauge how she was steering compared with us.

And if she wasn't there, as like as not he'd leave the coffee pot on the galley stove and go up to windward looking for her. Because he knew that when he got back to the forecastle, that would be the first thing they'd ask him – bleary-eyed and tousled, legs naked or in long underpants dangling over the upper bunk boards, or seated on the benches below –

'Where is she?' (Not where's *Herzogin*?)

'Abeam' (or it might 'ahead' or 'on the quarter')

'Which side?'

He'd point vaguely with the coffee pot, or with his other hand as he put the pot down on the table. They'd struggle from their bunks and flop down at the table, or slouch through the lee door and climb the rail, one hand on a backstay as they scanned the sea until they found her.

And so it would go on all day. Men painting on deck would look up occasionally to see where she'd got to. Or aloft in a bosun's chair, before shifting to a new position, you'd swing round to search the horizon. Cleaning out the pig-sty, coming up from the fore-peak with coal for the galley, or snatching up a draw-bucketful of water from overside, there'd always be time for a glance around. Were we gaining on her or falling back?

Among the people aft it was different. Not only John Mattson, but all three mates knew Sven Erikson personally. For all of them, therefore, it was personalities that counted more than ships. They'd think of *Herzogin* as 'he', the captain, rather than 'she', the ship. The contest was thus a personal one between their calm, steady and always dependable Captain, who seldom raised his voice, and dashing, thrusting, rip-roaring young Sven Erikson.

There were many tales of Sven's exploits; some of them brilliant, some of them violent; great feats of seamanship and courage; fights and furious rows in harbour; fast passages at sea; and always in the background the romantic figure of Pamela, who sailed with him and eventually became his wife.

Saturday, April 1st (Latitude 18° 38'S. Wind NNE)
The South East Trade Wind has been blowing from well to the north of east for the past five days. Last night we saw the Great Bear, so yet another stage in the voyage is behind us.

Sunday, April 2nd
For thirty-six hours the wind has headed us, giving *Herzogin*, who can sail half a point closer to it than we, a chance to catch up. She has been in sight all day – between ten and fifteen miles away on our port quarter.

Monday, April 3rd
Herzogin was on our weather quarter at dawn, and when the afternoon sun shone on her, it was possible to see through glasses that she had set sails on all her upper stays, including the upper of her two jigger topmast stays, so it's not surprising that she's caught up a little.

Tuesday, April 4th
Wind easterly. Light to moderate. Continuous rain. Course NNE. Excitement is growing. At dawn *Herzogin* was almost abeam. The old man decided to set a spare staysail on the upper jigger topmast stay. But *Herzogin* seems to have made a favourable slant out of this breeze and is slowly improving her position. There is talk of more staysails – one on each royal stay.

Wednesday, April 5th

It was thirty days ago that we first came in with *Herzogin* off the Horn. Then we saw no more of each other for nearly three weeks. But now, for the past ten days we've been sailing in company; first one and then the other seeking to windward or filling away to get the advantage of all sails drawing.

It's raining almost continuously, and the wind's shifting about. Surely we can't have reached the Doldrums yet, in latitude 8°S?

Thursday, April 6th

During the night, course was altered a point to the eastward in the hope of closing with *Herzogin*, and about two bells of the middle watch, in a clearing between two squalls, she suddenly appeared close aboard to starboard. Soon afterwards the next squall hid her, and when it cleared she was nowhere to be seen.

We came in with her again about noon. It was a day of flukey winds and almost continuous rain. Sometimes the squall clouds came to us from abeam or from aft. The ship would lie over and rush ahead, and when the rain cleared we'd perhaps have gained a mile or two, while *Herzogin* lay motionless with sails slatting, the squall having missed her.

Then, maybe, ten minutes later, a thick curtain of rain would hide her from us, and when it lifted we'd see her away ahead, with a stiff breeze in her sails, while we lay only just steering. However, when it grew dark our positions hadn't altered very much; maybe we were a mile or two closer, but one fresh squall could easily double (or cancel) the distance between us.

Friday, April 7th

At dawn the rain cleared again and ... 'There she is', shouted the first man to see her, well out on the starboard quarter.

Yes, during the night we'd sailed past her, and hopes ran high again that we were going to win this race. All through the forenoon the wind held fair – from about E by N – and blew fresh into the bargain. We sailed away from *Herzogin* so easily that by noon she was only just in sight astern. Then the wind hauled forward again, and we knew that she could hold us on that point of sailing.

Saturday, April 8th

Two steamers passed us bound north, both passenger ships, in constant communication with the outside world, and no doubt due shortly at some European port. For the past two months, the world for us has been uninhabited except by two tall ships – one white and powerful, the other long, slim, black and stately. The sight of the steamers seems to have affected us like the apple affected Adam and Eve. Tomorrow, I think, I shall have a shave.

Sunday, April 9th

Fernando Noronha abeam to port! The wind holds steady north-east-by-east, but very light. All day long we've had the tall cathedral rock of the main island in sight; and from the foretop one could just make out the upper sails of *Herzogin* on the eastern horizon. Later in the day she disappeared to windward, and we may not see her again. We've sailed over three thousand miles practically together and there's another three thousand miles ahead of us to Queenstown.

17.

Happy Easter

Wednesday, April 12th
Gradually the sky has become overcast, and yesterday evening the wind began to back. The ship was put about, and now at last we're sailing North with a fair wind. In continuous blinding rain, but who cares? It's the seventieth day out and we're north of the equator at last.

Saturday, April 15th
Yesterday was Good Friday, but today would be a working day if the skipper hadn't made us a present of it to square up in the forecastle. Everything is cleared out and piled on the hatches, which soon look like stalls at a jumble sale.

At sunset the Captain sent bottles of Aquavit forward to the forecastle and the petty officers' messes. Soon Sandholm's fiddle was out and Leimbach was joining in with his concertina. It was a brilliant night, with a light north-easterly breeze and splashes of moonlight moving here and there over the decks as the ship rose and subsided in the swell. There was dancing and singing, but not due to drink; there wasn't enough of it for that. More from a general feeling of relaxation, like Sunday in harbour.

All at once there came a loud roar, then a hush. People stood back in silent groups, anxious or expectant according to their natures. Where Koskinen had got the liquor from was a mystery. Either he'd smuggled a bottle aboard, or he'd been saving up his tots from earlier in the voyage.

To give him his due, Koskinen was meticulously courteous, well-behaved and responsible when sober. It was easy to imagine him commanding a naval patrol boat, or even a destroyer. But now he wasn't sober, he was roaring, rollicking drunk and lurching down the deck, singing a warlike song, with his knife out. And one didn't need two guesses as to where he was heading.

'Come out! Come out you Satan's Åland devil!' he roared in Finnish, and then in a mixture of Swedish and Finnish.

The door of the sailmaker's cabin crashed open, and there stood Berglund, white and stony with fury. He grabbed the huge teak grating from in front of the cuddy doorway (it weighed more than a hundredweight; I know because I had the job of lifting it back next morning) and brought it down with all his strength on Koskinen's head, felling him like an ox.

He lay there with blood pouring out of a deep gash on his forehead, where the edge of the grating had caught him. But a few moments later he was up again, blood streaming down his face ... and laughing ... roaring with laughter as he staggered about.

The officer of the watch – it was the Third Mate – paused in his pacing of the poop, looking down impassively, then turned and continued his pacing.

A little later, the skipper came down the ladder, followed nervously by the steward with a bowl of water and towels. Berglund barged back into his cabin without a word and slammed the door. The Skipper grabbed hold of Koskinen and started sloshing water in his face and mouth as he bellowed and bawled. Then he took a towel, threw it over the fellow's head and gave him a great shove in the back.

Koskinen went away forward in a staggering rush that ended at his bunk in the forecastle. He fell into it, and a moment later was sound asleep. In the morning he was his old sunny self, apparently remembering nothing of the night before and wondering how he'd got that great gash on his forehead. It was Easter Day. The sun was shining and the ship sailing merrily northwards over a glittering sea. Yes, it was a happy Easter for all of us. Even for Berglund, I suspect.

Sunday, April 16th (Lat. 05°07'N. Long. 38°42'W)
The Trade Wind goes on blowing, light but steady, and so we creep northwards under brilliant skies and over a calm blue sea, which at night turns black and mysterious in the light of a blazing moon. During the day we bask in the sunshine; at night we lie on our backs gazing dumbly at the stars. It's over eight days since we last saw *Herzogin*.

The bitter cold of the Southern Ocean, high winds and seas, the rain and sleet, strong head winds after the Horn, then stifling rain and calms in the doldrums – all these are in the past, and the future's not worth worrying about. Someday we must make land; until then, so long as she steers we're happy.

Saturday, April 29th (Lat. 24°02'. Long. 49°09'W)
Early this morning it fell calm. The mate, fishing from the bowsprit, hooked a good-sized Blue Marlin and managed to get it aboard. Soon all hands, including the Captain, were up forward fishing. There was a small shoal of Angel Fish. We caught seven or eight of these and a bream as well as another Blue Marlin, so we had an excellent fresh fish supper. There's thick Sargasso weed round the ship, full of animal life – sea lice and small crabs skittering about. The Southern Cross is still clearly visible just above the horizon at midnight.

Sunday, April 30th
Two of the lads stand facing each other on the foredeck. They've fought themselves to a standstill and can only glare with undiminished ferocity, muscular arms hanging

limp but ready, broad sun-bronzed backs with muscles playing up and down at each slight movement.

What it's all about nobody knows. They may even have forgotten themselves. They continue to stand there for close on fifteen minutes, hard grey eyes glaring out of bruised and battered faces, each too proud to be the first to move.

Quite suddenly the wind freshens, the ship lies over and all eyes, including theirs, turn to windward. Within half an hour the ship is snoring along at ten knots. Clouds of spray are flying across the deck and all quarrels are forgotten.

Monday, May 1st (Lat. 27°23'N. Long. 53°03'W.)
Wind easterly, moderate to fresh. A family of rats has settled in the forecastle. They have become so tame that repeated attempts by Axel West to catch them by the tail don't seem to bother them. They rather like him, and unless he makes a sudden grab, they don't run away.

A solitary white light was seen to windward during the first watch. Was it the stern light of a sailing vessel – *Herzogin* or *Mozart*, maybe? Or could it be a raft with survivors? No flares or anything. Anyway we couldn't possibly reach them so far to windward, and we have no means of reporting. At dawn two of the watch went up to the main royal yard to search the horizon, but nothing could be seen.

Saturday, May 6th (Lat. 41°00'N. Long. 38°18'W.)
Wind SW fresh. The barometer is falling and the wind has freshened from south-west. In the afternoon it veered to north-west and increased steadily in strength. By midnight there was quite a sea running and green water beginning to come aboard again for the first time in many weeks. Less than 1500 miles to Queenstown.

Tuesday, May 9th (Lat. 45°36'N. Long. 29°09'W.)
Wind SW, speed 11 knots. We trimmed 75 sacks of wheat from starboard to port in the forehold. Our third pig was killed and with any luck we shall raise land before the fresh meat runs out. This is the 98th day of the voyage. Looks like being a smart passage. But where are *Herzogin* and *Mozart*?

Thursday, May 11th (Lat. 48°04'N. Long. 23°44'W.)
Wind WSW. Yesterday at noon we had 864 miles left, today about 700, and still the wind holds fair, bringing with it wet weather and mist. There's quite a fever of making and mending aboard. Suitcases are being painted outrageous colours. Almost everyone is at work on his canvas shoes or fancy belt or sea chest handles, and every evening we gather round the man who's been calculating the day's run and the distance to Queenstown from a chit given him by the second mate.

They salted down most of that pig before we'd had more than one square meal of it. But who cares, with the green hills of home so close ahead.

Saturday, May 13th
Wind WSW. Light. Thick fog. Visibility nil. The weather has been thick all day, but the wind keeps westerly, though light. We creep along with the high mournful wail of our foghorn crying into the mist around us. During the forenoon we set up the fish tackle from the fore cross-trees, ready to sling the anchors. At noon we were little more than 300 miles from Queenstown.

Sunday, May 14th
The breeze, such as it was, held steady all night and towards morning began to freshen from south-east. By noon we were making 6 knots, and a glimpse of the sun gave the skipper a

chance to check the latitude. We're now about 130 miles from Queenstown, and 25 or so from Cape Clear.

That's going to be our problem. We're a bit too far north, sailing clean full on a south-easterly wind. Will we weather the Fastnet, or have to come about? If so, it might mean beating this way and that for days yet. And *Herzogin* further south maybe, having a clear run into harbour?

During the day there were many signs of our approach to land. Some herring gulls kept us company during the afternoon, and later on we put up a pair of gannets. Again and again we counted the hours, tried to judge the speed and looked hopefully at a leaden sky. A shift of half a point more easterly in the wind could mean disaster. If we fetched even a mile or so to leeward of the Fastnet – or a hundred yards, for that matter – it would be 'About ship!' and away out again into the grey Atlantic.

Many walked the deck that evening, and early in the first watch we got a shock. 'Clear lower braces for running. ... Overhaul royal and to'gallant braces.'

It hit us like a rock. We were going about then. After all our hopes. The watch below threw their cards on the table and abandoned the game they were playing. The magnitude of the tragedy sent all other thoughts and interests flying.

We imagined *Herzogin* watching, from well to windward, as always, and passing Cape Clear with a comfortable offing. We thought of ourselves with land almost in sight, yet doomed to stand off to seaward, perhaps for a week or more. We waited dismally for the dreaded 'Ready About!' But it didn't come. Instead an additional look-out was posted in the fore cross-trees. A light rain was falling and visibility had become poor.

Monday, May 15th

Everyone's on edge. Frederikson, the mate, comes forward at the end of the afternoon watch to trim sails. He's a bit unsteady on his feet; they've been drinking aft, I dare say.

But I'm not prepared for a thump in the seat of my pants as I turn to go forward. 'Get a move on,' he growls in Swedish.

This is too much. I round on him, and one or two others close in behind me. Frederikson grabs a belaying pin from the rail and swipes me across the mouth. I'm furious and go for him, spitting blood and half an eye tooth. But the others get between us fast.

The wind has freshened, and we see now that John Mattson was simply being cautious, as ever. The braces had to be overhauled in case a sudden manoeuvre were forced upon him, so close to land and in a busy steamer lane.

Then at 10.15 p.m. comes the sweetest sound of the whole voyage, a hail from the look-out aloft of 'Light broad on the port bow'. We've weathered the Fastnet!

We raised Daunt's Rock Light, off Queenstown, 104 days out from Aussie ... a reasonably good passage ... But for us this was of less importance ... We crowded round the pilot as he climbed aboard:

'Boys,' he said, 'You've done well! ... Only three other ships in so far, and you've beaten 'em all.'

We hardly heard him. 'Where's *Herzogin*?' we clamoured.

'Still at sea.'

The shout that went up must have carried far into the hills and mountains.

Part IV
Islands and Islanders

18.

The Sun at Midnight

Herzogin reached Falmouth five days later, we heard eventually; but by then we were well up Channel, bound for Hull.

We slipped out of Queenstown under tow at dawn on Tuesday, May 23rd. The air was breathless as the sun climbed over the hill and burst on the sleeping harbour. The sky was cloudless. Houses and barracks shone brightly in the early sunlight. As we cleared the narrows, *Viking* came up to Daunt Rock and anchored, 107 days out from Port Victoria.

It turned into a glorious hot spring day with a light westerly breeze, but at sunset the wind freshened, and before midnight we raised the Bishop Rock light fine on the port bow. Next morning the Scillies lay spread over the sea to the north of us, then Land's End, and in the evening we passed the Lizard, with little Cadgwith tucked snugly into the cliffs behind it. I wondered whether Sheila and her family – both her families – still went there. Not as early in the year as this anyway.

The wind hauled northerly and grew stronger. At midnight we passed Start Point, and soon after daybreak we had the Needles abeam, then St Catherine's Point. It being Ascension Day we had a holiday, and it truly was a joy to be alive – striding up Channel with white sails standing stiff and full above us in brilliant sunshine, and the scent of spring grass and flowers coming out to us on a fresh beam wind.

Great liners and cargo steamers altered course to pass us close. We saw destroyers and a cruiser, and once a seaplane circled round us. During the forenoon also we overtook a steamer; and a large cruising yacht of curious rig sailed after us all day, but failed to catch us.

Each well-remembered headland, every gleaming cliff seemed to welcome us. The Channel was full of ships – Swedes, Danes, Germans, Frenchmen, British – and the crews of lightships cheered us as we passed. From Selsey Bill to Seaford and on to Beachy Head, the hills and beacons came down to the sea to greet us.

As we passed the Royal Sovereign, the sun turned fire red and dived into a bank of purple haze lying round the horizon. At midnight we passed close inshore at Dungeness, where flashes from the lighthouse swept our sails, sweeping us on our way.

When we were still a few miles west of Dover, the wind suddenly freshened, and we shot past into the North Sea with water spouting up through our lee scupper holes. A little later we rounded the South Goodwin Light Vessel '*á craquer un oeuf*', as M. Paitry used to say.

Then began a hard beat up the North Sea. By 8 o'clock next morning we were abreast of the North Hinder Light Vessel, off the mouth of the Scheldt. Here we put about. There was a moderate breeze with no sea to speak of; she came round like a 5-ton yawl. Off the mouth of the London river we tacked again, and at seven that evening the liner *Bremen* appeared out of the mist to starboard. She passed close astern of us and dipped her ensign in salute. Her passengers cheered. We dipped and cheered back.

It is difficult, in a few words, to describe that lovely ship – gone now, like the *Olivebank* herself. We were lying almost becalmed as she swept by with a roar from her great bow wave, a low rumble of powerful machinery and the singing of generators, through which the thin high cheering of her passengers sounded small and distant. She passed us at a distance hardly greater than her own length, throwing a green bow wave higher than our own poop deck, yet scarcely a ripple disturbed the water alongside us.

Two days later, a tug picked us up off Spurn Head and towed us into the Humber.

I was able to spend a couple of weeks at home, but everyone I knew seemed to be away. Sheila and John had gone down to Cornwall early, and one of my closest boyhood friends was languishing in a Swiss sanatorium. They said he'd become an air swallower, which sounded harmless enough, but apparently he nearly died of it.

However, Lasse came down with me, and we were joined later by Chrisse von Frenckel, an old schoolmate of his. We had rather an interesting week from my point of view, because Chrisse wanted to see all sorts of historic places that I'd never been to myself. The Tower of London and Runnymede were two of them, I remember. But the day Lasse and I left to rejoin *Olivebank*, I was feeling lousy. I put it down to over-indulgence in rich foods after a year at sea. My mother had a theory about fresh cream.

A brown shark followed us out to sea from the Yorkshire coast, but no-one took any notice as they hurried about making sail for the last time. *Olivebank* had been a year away – two years from Finland – and now she was homeward bound for the Baltic at last. A moderate south-westerly carried us along at ten or eleven knots under a cloudy sky, and all that night the lights of fishing boats, bobbing and blinking on the Dogger Bank, kept us company. I wondered whether *Woolbyrne* was at sea too.

All the way over from the Humber to Skagerak I still felt rotten. I don't remember what winds we had, but they must have been light, because it took us a full week to reach Copenhagen. And for the last four days of that passage I was a source of considerable amusement and speculation owing to the remarkable colour of my water. A lively lemon yellow it was at first, and later an attractive shade of orange. No cabaret artist ever commanded a more enthusiastic or interested audience than I did, two or three times a day, when my watch was called and we all went to the rail to 'ease springs'.

The Donkeyman said it was yellow fever, and since he was an old shellback of thirty-one (most of the rest of us were in our early twenties) his opinion carried a great deal of weight. 'By Damn!' he shouted, gazing with interest and admiration at the brilliant saffron stream I was projecting into the sea. 'There's only one ting for dat ... one spoon Stockholm tar (*trä tjära*) with stockfish soaked in rum.'

This and other remedies were tried without effect. Few people in those days (and certainly no-one on board) had heard of *hepatitis,* so my malady went undiagnosed, except by the Donkeyman, for the whole of that passage. And by the time we raised the Åland Islands – two weeks out from England – I had begun to feel better.

It was early June, and in Latitude 59° North there was no real night. For the past twenty-four hours there'd been no wind in the Baltic either. The ship stood upright and very still, as though spellbound. No swell moved; not a rattle or creak from aloft.

I was on day work, though still feeling a bit weak, so I turned in early. But around midnight Lasse called me on deck. I came out blinking.

The northern horizon was aglow, and a little to the west of north a crimson tongue of cloud, like a dying flame, showed where the sun had set. A slight breeze had sprung up. The ship was forging gently north-eastward over a black sea – jet black, like lake water, and faintly ruffled where the breeze caught it. No swell, no movement, and not a sound except the lazy flap of a sail just lifting overhead.

A schooner and a small timber barque (her name was *Sverre*, I remember. She's gone now.) stood pointing in opposite directions, like cardboard cut-outs against the after-glow. And between them, two short dark strokes, as though drawn by a carpenter's pencil on the horizon. That was what they looked like – two hyphens on a bowl of ink. It was Lågskär, one of the outer skerries of the Åland Islands; and all down the ship's side men stood watching – expressionless and silent – not sailors any more, just Finns.

For another hour the dusk persisted. Then a little to the east of north the sky began to gleam, then glow, then turn to flame. At the same time a breath of wind came down to us out of the forests, heavy with the scent of pines. The horizon ahead had become a continuous black line, rough-edged where the tops of pine trees stood out against the dawn.

At noon we entered harbour, with pine forests all round us. I was feeling well for the first time in weeks; nevertheless they sent me off to hospital – a little white-painted cottage hospital among the trees, where a sister and a nurse looked after eight beds. I was the only patient, and for ten days I did absolutely nothing but eat and sleep and ring bells for my slightest need – mainly company. I luxuriated in the quiet, the peace, the sound of birds and the long deep sighs of the pine trees.

Olivebank paid off and some of my friends came to see me before dispersing to their homes. Lasse came with Sandholm. They were off to Helsingfors by steamer that evening – travelling together, though they were never close friends. But life ashore can be strange and rather disturbing for the first few days after years away. So shipmates tend to keep together at first, for company.

Vuori came alone. He seemed a bit subdued. I knew he'd decided to sit for 2nd Mate, and maybe he feared that this would de-bar him from continuing in the ships he loved: hardly any of Erikson's officers were non-Ålanders in those days.

We chatted for a while. Then he brightened ' ... Let's meet in twenty years from today,' he said 'and see who's served the longest in sail.' And so it was agreed: at noon on June 15th, 1954, we'd meet at Charlie Brown's, in London's East End (Vuori always had a great affection for the place), and whoever had served the least in sail would buy all the drinks.

Sadly it never happened. Ragnar Vuori got his ticket and *was* taken on by Erikson. He was serving as first mate of *Olivebank* in September 1939 when, crossing the Dogger Bank on her way home to Finland, she struck an enemy mine and sank at once. She settled on the bottom, but one of her masts still stood, with its royal and to'gallant yards a few feet above the surface. Seven men clung to them and were picked up two days later by a Danish trawler. Vuori wasn't one of them. The last anyone saw of him, he was hanging onto an empty fresh water tank which had somehow floated free from *Olivebank*'s shattered hold. Perhaps it sank, or Vuori got tired or lost his grip. He was never seen again.

But he won the wager. By 1954 I had only served six years in those and other sailing ships. Vuori must have served twelve at least.

Gunnar Sandbolm and Axel West came together. Axel had brought a bottle of Brännvin in his mackintosh pocket. *Olivebank* would be laid up all summer, they told me – from now until October. I decided at once that I must find a boat, in which I could sail round the islands and look in on some of the boys. Would that be possible? Of course it would; boats were cheap and plentiful in Finland and people were always building themselves new ones. But meanwhile, how about another drink?

The doctor had been very stern on the subject of animal fats. 'For three months' he said 'no fat meats of any kind, no butter, no cheese, only chicken without its skin and fish – as much as you can eat.' And I think anything spicy was out too. But there was no mention of drink, not a word; so it sounded as though the next three or four months before the ships signed on again were going to be quite a party.

Meanwhile there seemed to be a bit of a party building up among the pine trees in the hospital grounds. I hastened to join in. There were one or two more Olivebankers there and a few from other ships, with their girlfriends or come to chat up the nurses. Jan Lindqvist had brought his sister Elsa. Granö's Elsa – Pine Island's Elsa – they called her.

She was small and blonde and very beautiful, with green eyes which had a quizzical, half-mocking look in them. She was dressed in a pale skirt and blouse, brown shoes, no stockings and a dark linen coat, a bit too long in the sleeves. Her blonde hair was roughly crammed into a white knitted cap perched on the back of her head.

She looked adorable sitting there talking quietly to her brother. But it was the contrast between her schoolgirlish get-up and a harsh, husky voice and strong hands, roughened by hard work, that really intrigued me.

And when she rose and moved away, it was like a bursting into song. There was poetry in every stride, in every twist and turn. Leaping across a small stream to meet a friend, her linen coat flew wide, the skirt twirled and flared, revealing shapely legs and thighs. It was a bewitching sight.

Next day I left hospital and went straight to Erikson's office for my back pay. It amounted to £27, which was quite a lot in Finland in those days. Gunnar Sandblom, of Hangö, and Eric Lindbolm, both *Olivebank* ABs, were there too. Eric lived in Mariehamn itself. 'Where are you going to stay?' he asked. I hadn't thought much about it. 'You'd better come to us, we've got a spare room and mother likes me to have friends.'

Eric and I had been in the same watch in *Olivebank*. He was rather a pretty-looking chap with apple cheeks, but manly in every other way and a prime seaman. I soon discovered why his mother liked him to bring home friends; it was because he was the youngest of a family of four, all girls except himself.

One day there was a fair with dancing, over in the eastern harbour. And suddenly there was Elsa, with that slightly mocking expression on her face.

'You don't dance, Elsa?'

'I like to talk and maybe drink a little.'

'With sailors?'

I knew it was a silly question, but she gave it some thought, and then said ' ... life in Åland never changes ... sailors know other lives.'

'But isn't dancing more fun?'

'Dancing leads to trouble ... sometimes fighting, sometimes loving.'

'And what's wrong with loving?'

She looked up, smiling,: 'You ask because you wish to know ... or only tell what you want?'

That was difficult to answer, so I didn't try. We walked on for a bit in silence. Then she said ... 'Summer is time for loving ... and fighting ... winter for forgetting ... ' She paused, looking thoughtful, then added 'Fighting is easier to forget.'

We strolled on through the fairground, stopping at stalls here and there. Elsa seemed happy enough chatting to her friends – sometimes on her own, sometimes bringing me in. There were games to play, things to buy, things to eat, beer and spirits, ice creams. We tried our strength or skills at various stalls, and laughed a lot. Till all at once, as suddenly as she'd come, Elsa was gone.

Then there was the seamstress with big brown eyes, who lived alone with her baby daughter in a little wooden house among birch trees on the outskirts of town. She also liked picnics in the forest and intimate little afternoons at home. But Eric's sisters didn't approve of seamstresses, it seemed; they were never any better than they ought to be, which was really only a round-about way of saying they didn't like this one.

Anyway how good *ought* seamstresses to be, we wanted to know. But the situation was becoming difficult. It was time to move on again. I longed to get out into the islands, where several of my shipmates had homes within a few miles of Mariehamn.

Jan Lindqvist sent word by his elder brother to say that I could live in their boat-house for a week or two, if I liked, and help with the fishing; the ströming were running strong this year.

Then one day, he and Elsa came into town again with a boat full of fish, in casks and boxes for the market. They brought word of a boat for sale on one of the outer islands. If I liked her I could fit her out alongside their jetty in Granö. This sounded great, but I don't remember any more about that evening. All I do remember is waking up next morning in a bunk bed in the corner of a small low-ceilinged room.

At a wood stove on the other side of the room a woman was cooking. Through the open door I could see an elderly man seated on a barrel, mending nets. I had never seen either of them before as far as I knew, but I recognised vaguely the face of a younger man who now came in: he had been at last night's party.

'You are looking for a boat?' he asked.

'Was I? Oh, yes.' My head was buzzing like a band saw, which seemed to be cutting it in half down the middle.

We went outside, and there, hauled up just clear of the water, was an eighteen foot sailing boat, complete with mast and sails. In fact, the main sprit-sail was set, and swinging gently from side to side in random puffs of wind from across the fjord.

She was a sturdy little open fishing boat with a curved stem and a transom stern. She had a short mast, which you stepped through a hole in the forward thwart, and a sprit heeled in a strop on the mast. Her only defect was that she had no rudder; you steered with an oar dropped into a groove on the transom; and in case of need there was a short lanyard to hold it down. This could also be an advantage, though, because if the wind died, or you misjudged when coming alongside, you were all set to scull her in with the steering oar.

She was just what I wanted. I loved her on sight. 'How much?' I asked.

'What about two thousand, seven hundred marks?'

I couldn't believe it. I knew nothing (hadn't even heard) of the rampant Finnish inflation of those days, which was to result very soon in revaluation. All I knew was that in English money at that time she would cost me three pounds, seven shillings and sixpence. There must be something wrong with her.

But there wasn't. She was in prime condition. And I could build a cabin in her as soon as I could get hold of some timber and tools. Eventually we launched her into the fjord, and that evening, after baling her out, I sailed for Mariehamn through the islands.

19.

The Scent Of Pines

It was a thrilling moment. I'd never owned a boat before. I called her *Lilla Vän* (Little Friend), and that was what she was. I now had someone else to think about and look after. It was a new experience.

Kalle Björklund, who'd sold her to me, had also helped me to stock her up with bread, milk, eggs, cheese, butter (damn the doctor), coffee, salt, pepper, sugar, potatoes, a primus stove, kettle, frying pan and a can of water – all stowed in lockers under the transom seat or under the spare jib forward. And just before I left, the old man had brought a small trammel net out of his shed and laid it over *Lilla Vän*'s forward thwart.

It still lay there, carefully flaked down, ready for shaking out over the side. So I thought I'd try my luck in a sheltered creek which appeared between two islands. I struck the mainsail and sculled the boat into the narrows (Plate 15), where I managed with some difficulty to lay the net across between the islands, anchoring it with stones at either end. Then I hauled the boat half out of the water, onto a scrap of shingle beach between rocks, on one side of the creek, and tied the painter to a tree.

I slept fitfully through the dusk hours, on the mainsail and jib piled in the bottom of the boat, with the spare jib over me. Loud skutterings and splashing from shoals of eider duck and scoter kept breaking in upon the stillness, and once I was wakened by a loud bellowing – something between a boom and a roar. I stood up in the boat and saw, silhouetted against the afterglow, on a bare dome of rock emerging from trees near the top of the island, a large bull elk, bawling his head off into the gloaming. After a while I could hear grunting and splashing out in the creek, and a cow elk came swimming over. She heaved herself out of the water not far from the boat and disappeared into the pines. I heard them crashing around for quite a time after that, but ultimately I fell asleep.

When I woke again the sun was well up. I sculled the boat over to my net and found a small green pike trapped in one of the pockets. So poor a catch would no doubt have disappointed Kalle, but it delighted me. I had fried fish for breakfast, with bread which was still quite fresh, lots of butter and coffee. This was the life, I thought. It seemed hardly worthwhile sailing all the way back to Mariehamn. And if it hadn't been for the need to build some kind of cabin against the dew and the rain (Plate 16), which must come eventually, I don't think I would have troubled.

When I reached Mariehamn my first concern was to buy tools and timber. All I needed were some 4" x ½" tongued-and-grooved planks, some plywood for locker doors and 2" x 2"s for beams and framework. It took me nearly three weeks to get everything firmly secured in its right place, with a mixture of pitch and Stockholm tar in all the cabin-top joints, and a painted canvas cover over the lot. Then a few shelves, some lockers for stores and a simple bunk, and I was ready for sea.

I didn't lack for advice. Boatbuilders never do. There are always a few loafers or passers-by who like to lean on the gunwale for a while, with an occasional 'Ah ...' or 'H'm' or 'If I were you ...'. But I seemed to have a permanent audience, and not only of small boys. Elsa and Jan came once a week on their way to market, and again in the evening. The Lindblom girls – two sisters and a cousin – attended in force most days, and took me home afterwards.

Even my seamstress friend wandered down one Saturday morning, and poked her head into the cabin, which was nearly finished.

'You'll be lonely in that little bunk.'

'Not for long' I said stupidly. She went off in a huff, and I felt ashamed.

Then Captain Mattson came. He was in Mariehamn waiting appointment to another ship. So *Olivebank* was to have a new master. I wondered what he'd be like.

Mattson asked to be taken for a sail and, like all good captains, he was an excellent crew – calm and attentive as always and completely relaxed. We tacked down the fjord for a mile or so, then ran back to where *Olivebank* lay at anchor. 'You will become Ålänning?' he said, as we came alongside.

'I want to get my tickets in sail. After that I'll see.'

'Sailing ships soon will be gone ... If you do not like steamers, better to be a farmer.'

'Ålanders are both, aren't they?'

'Yes, or neither. Technik is gripping on all of us.'

'Not on me, I hope. Jan Lindqvist says I can sleep in their boat-house. I'm sailing down there as soon as I'm stored up.'

John Mattson looked at me seriously, but his eyes were smiling. 'Take care,' he said. 'These fjords are not easy. There can be rocks in the deepest channels.'

'I think I can manage.'

'Take care,' he repeated. 'Follow the beacons. If you miss one, turn back ... turn back at once and anchor, then fix your position.'

I sailed one evening towards midnight. The sun had just set. *Lilla Vän* swam silently between the trees, under mainsail only, before a faint land breeze. The scent of pines rolled after us as I followed the main channel southwards.

I can still feel today the elation, the sense of fulfilment that swept through me. I heard the purring of blackcock from somewhere in the forest to port. Then I saw what looked like the branch of a dead tree moving across the fjord ahead of me; but it wasn't a branch, it was the antlers of an elk swimming – maybe the very one I'd seen a few weeks ago.

Soon the fairway divided. I chose the eastern arm and sailed on. It was now nearly dark – as dark as it gets up there in summer. I had to use my flash-lamp to follow the chart on my knees, switching it off from time to time to check on the beacons marking the channel. It was sometimes difficult to make them out, but I stood on hopefully; and a little later, from away to starboard, the old elk bellowed – also hopefully.

Fellow-feeling made me smile: questing through the night to my lady, as he to his – or words to that effect. In my imagination, I saw Elsa greeting me with pleasure, perhaps even with admiration. I suppose I got a bit carried away by the idea, and needed bringing down to earth; because, as the fjord widened, the land receded on either hand, and all at once, without the background of dark rock and pines to show them up, the beacons vanished.

'Turn back, turn back at once', John Mattson had said. But I couldn't. I just couldn't throw away my dream like that: the smiling face at dawn, and laughing eyes and the thrill of making them shine.

The wind had gone easterly, but there was still a light breeze. I stood on and stood on, in a more or less southerly direction, keeping as well as I could to the middle of the fjord ... till suddenly the keel grated loudly, the bows lifted and the boat stopped dead, listing heavily to starboard. We were hard aground.

At first, as I peered into the semi-darkness around me, I felt stunned. Then horribly afraid, for *Lilla Vän* and for myself. The land looked far away on both sides, and the wind was freshening.

I tried to think calmly. In deference to John Mattson's

warning, I had brought the anchor aft, outboard of all, into the cockpit, with four or five fathoms of warp turned up on a cleat forward. I took off my jacket and tossed it into the cabin. Then, carrying the anchor in one hand and clinging to the gunwale with the other, I lowered myself over the side ... and immediately took heart: with the weight of myself and the anchor out of her, *Lilla Vän* lifted a little and bumped.

Her stern was in deep water: my feet had found no bottom. It wasn't until I'd worked my way forward almost to her bow that I struck anything solid, and a moment later was standing on a shelf of hard rock with the water up to my knees. *Lilla Vän* had grounded on an outcrop, on the very edge of the shoal: a few feet further west and she'd have missed it altogether!

She bumped again. I dropped the anchor, put my back and shoulders to her port bow and shoved with all my might. She bumped again ... and again ... and again ... and slid off! And, to my horror, with a horrible grating and clanking, the anchor went with her. I plunged madly into the sea, grabbed for her gunwale and missed. Then she was gone.

My greatest error, of course, was not to have struck her sail. But it also wasn't very clever just to fling the anchor down without checking to see if it would hold. Anyway, there was nothing for it now but to seek out the shallowest part of the reef and stay there till another boat came by – if boats ever did come that way.

For a while I floundered about, barking my shins and ankles on submerged rocks, until I eventually managed to scramble onto a sort of plateau which was almost awash. There I stood, as lonely as a cormorant and every bit as stupid-looking, with surf all round me and the wind still freshening. From somewhere in the north-west the old elk bellowed again loudly. The sound depressed me.

There is seldom any rise and fall in the level of the Baltic, and never more that a foot or two. So, unless any real weather blew up, and heavy seas began sweeping the reef, I'd be unlikely to drown. But the shame of it! The thought of being found there in the morning, like an orphan child in a snowstorm – maybe by the kind Lindqvists themselves – was hard to bear.

A half moon rose uncertainly out of the mist in the east. Soon I could make out the land on the other side. It was nearer than I'd thought; not more than a mile at the most. On a sudden impulse I pulled off my trousers and flung them down. Then I plunged into the sea again, and struck out with renewed optimism and hope. Someone would see *Lilla Vän*. She wouldn't get far with her anchor down. She'd be found and I'd have her back before long.

That swim – possibly my longest ever – remains only vaguely in my mind. I had heard stories about boats found sailing on their own down the leads, and evil spirits who lived at the bottoms of lakes and fjords waiting to grab people as they swam or sailed by. I remember thinking back over a whole catalogue of misdeeds, which I now bitterly regretted, and bargaining silently with the Fates for my salvation and *Lilla Vän*'s.

After a while I began to tire and take less care about keeping my mouth and nose above water. I was getting to feel a bit light-headed, muddled and rather woozy ... when suddenly, out of nowhere, a pale apparition loomed up almost beside me. It was *Lilla Vän*. Her anchor, hanging in the water, must have dragged her into the wind again and again; to fill away on one side or the other, but drifting all the time steadily down wind to the west.

I grabbed at the anchor warp and hung on for dear life, panting and gasping, till at last I could find the strength to haul myself up, hand over hand to the gunwale, and finally aboard.

The sky was lightening in the east, the sun would soon be up. I struggled forward and lifted the anchor out of the water, then took the spare jib aft with me, to wrap around my bare legs and shirt tails. I was shivering violently.

But now, without the anchor hanging from her bow, *Lilla Vän* fell away to starboard, gathering way, and I was able to steer for what looked like a small inlet between two spurs of land on the western shore. Ten minutes later we ran in between those spurs and brought up in the lee of one of them.

Down went the anchor with a good fifteen fathoms of warp, and down came the sail. Then I tore off my soaking shirt and almost fell into the cabin. It was warm and dry in there. I rolled into my bunk and pulled two blankets and the spare jib over me. Within minutes I was asleep.

I was woken by the thump of a boat coming alongside, and the thunder of her screw thrashing astern. Then came the sound of a fist hammering on *Lilla Vän*'s cabin top. I clambered out, dragging the spare jib around me, and there, just as I'd imagined her, was Elsa. But not smiling exactly; more grinning from ear to ear.

Jan, at the wheel of their motor-boat, called out: 'What were you doing out there? Trying to teach your boat to waltz? We watched for a long time, but couldn't see you on board.'

'And we found these' grinned Elsa, holding up a dripping pair of trousers. 'Have you decided to do without them? ... I must tell the girls'.

20.

Green Leaf Harvest

I was so happy to see them that I could only grin back. They had been lifting nets and were on their way to market with the fish.

Elsa chucked my pants into *Lilla Vän*'s cockpit and bore off. She seemed to be in high spirits. Perhaps it was my bedraggled appearance and strange get up – like a seaside landlady in a dust sheet – that made her laugh.

Jan put his engine into gear and revved up. 'The boys'll be round soon to pilot you in,' he shouted, as they headed away up the fjord. Elsa waved energetically, and I waved back.

It was half-past five of a sparkling morning, with the sun well up and the faintest of easterly breezes just ruffling the surface of the fjord. I sculled *Lilla Vän* over to the nearest land and carried the anchor ashore, taking care to hook it well into to a crevice in the rocks. Then I got out the primus and set about making breakfast, while waiting for 'the boys' to show up.

When they did, I got a bit of a shock. A sailing boat, like *Lilla Vän* only bigger, came gliding round the point, and in her were two small boys – really small; I found out later that one was seven and the other five, yet they handled that big sailing boat as though they'd been born in her. Furthermore, they turned out to be the brothers of Jan and Elsa, who'd sent them round to look for me.

The Lindqvists' jetty and boat-house, with a net-house beside it, were on the other side of the point, and twenty minutes later *Lilla Vän* was safely moored. Up a short slope behind the boat house stood the Lindqvist family home – a weather-board cottage painted dark red, and double-skinned against the sub-arctic winter. It was set among apple trees, and the whole Lindqvist family lived there – father, mother, four boys and three girls.

How they all fitted in I don't know because, come to think of it, I never went inside; I lived in *Lilla Vän* and all family life, from early morning till late at night throughout the summer, seemed to be centred round the jetty, the boat-house, a cowshed and a small smoke-house, where Ragnar Lindqvist, Jan's 28-year-old brother, turned ströming into böckling and packed them into boxes for the market. It was a busy scene, and a busy, happy life for us all. I'd never met a family who could get through so much in one day, even when there were some twenty-three hours between dawn and dusk

First there was the ströming fishing. Every morning father Lindqvist, a man of about fifty with a cheerful red face and greying hair, and either Jan or Elsa, took their motor-boat out into the open sea south of the island, to haul the ströming nets which had been laid two days before. One day, when it was Elsa's turn, I went out with them.

At first I found it difficult to make myself useful. Elsa and the old man had everything weighed off. They knew exactly when and where to do what; I could only tag along after them, and often got in the way or did the wrong thing. In the end, I steered the boat and kept the engine just ticking over, or stopped, while they did the hauling and stowing.

They worked like demons, shouting and swearing, with every now and then a loud fart from one or other of them, which kept us all amused and happy. The Swedish swear words Fan (pronounced 'Fahn') and Satan ('Sahtan') have a resounding, and most satisfying violence, which places them in a class of their own for relief to one's feelings. Elsa flung them to the wind in great bellowing cadences every time the net snagged – or freed itself and sent her crashing into the bottom of the boat among the fish. Then she'd yell at me 'Hold her steady, för Satan, Seligman!' and grab the net again in those strong, rough hands of hers.

Elsa, although she was so small and slender, hauled a good deal heavier than I could have done. She knew exactly where to take hold and how much to lift before dragging. I watched her with envy as well as admiration; and tried again and again to equate the demure, rather shy little person one met in unfamiliar surroundings ashore, talking wistfully of love and eating ice-creams, with this boisterous, hard-working hard-swearing young fish-wife, handling nets and screeching helm orders in most unladylike language.

And a third picture, only a day or two before, when I'd suggested photographing the whole family in front of their house. They'd all assembled in their everyday clothes. Except Elsa, who was adrift somewhere, so we started without her. But I'd only taken one picture, when there she was, mincing down the pathway from the house. She couldn't have walked any other way, because she was dressed in an elaborate party frock, which followed the line of her body almost down to her ankles. And for once she'd left off her white knitted cap. Instead, her blonde hair was carefully combed and oiled till it shone like gold. She looked strangely out-of-place on that rocky hillside, and quite enchanting.

The ströming were running in long shoals, and almost every day the nets would come in alive with them – a squirming silvery carpet of fish that filled the bottom of the boat. Then all other work ashore would be dropped, and all hands – male and female – would be turned to gutting the catch, which had been scooped out of the boat into a large square vat on the jetty.

We all gathered round this vat on stools or tubs. And people would come in from round about – even from other islands – to help. It was a highly skilled job, which they seemed to do with a single twist of the finger per fish. You then threw the gutted fish into a small cask beside you, which was periodically sprinkled with coarse salt by little sister Hjördis. I was very slow at this, and the salt got into cuts in my fingers. Everyone was chatting or laughing and there was lots of 'spreet'; every hour or so Mrs Lindqvist would come striding down the slope from the house, plump and smiling, with a fresh bottle in her hands. People came and went. Usually someone brought an accordion. Then there'd be singing, and later on – when the ströming vat was empty and most of the casks filled – there'd be dancing too, sometimes till dawn.

Those were uproarious days and nights; but you had to know how to handle them. I didn't at first, and I remember one night getting into such a frenzy of joy and intoxication that I started hammering the solid timber doors of the boat-house with my bare fists. In fact, two of us had a bet on which could break the door down first. Neither of us could. And hell it was for the next week or so, with barked and bruised knuckles that simply would not heal. Too much 'spreet' in the blood, I suppose.

Throughout the summer, while the ströming were running, there'd be gutting parties somewhere almost every night. Soon I got the hang of keeping a full glass out in front, that couldn't be added to, and another at my feet for occasional sips.

Hjördis was a remarkable child. Just ten and possessed of phenomenal energy. You'd see her all day any day, with her tousled brown hair, brown eyes and wearing a nondescript sort of cotton dress with a faded pattern, darting among the nets hung up to dry, back and forth to the floating fish cages moored to the jetty, or rowing hard across the fjord in her little 'eker' rowing boat – her own, no-one else was allowed to use it.

She'd always have the boat piled up with nets – a dozen or more – which she'd lay in the evening, in channels where she knew the roach and perch moved about. Sometimes one of her young brothers went with her, to keep the boat moving while she shook the nets out into the water and moored one end with a stone. Sometimes she managed on her own.

In the morning she'd be out again early to lift the nets, bring back the fish to the cages and hang the nets up. When they were dry, she'd start cleaning them, pulling out bits of weed and muck which would make them visible and therefore avoidable by fish in the water. She seldom spoke, but occasionally she'd give you a quick glance and half a smile, as much as to say: 'There. That'll do to be going on with. Now, what's next?' And off she'd go, here and there, wrenching and hauling or hammering and digging, whatever was needed.

When the weather was right she would go out with a throwing line and spinner for pike. Pelle, the seven-year-old, usually went with her, and once I joined them in *Lilla Vän*. When we got to where Hjördis knew there were fish, we hauled our boats out and started fishing from a bit of stony beach. I moved off and went to the top of a low cliff nearby. 'No good,' said Hjördis. 'You lose fish.'

Of course I knew better. I swung my spinner round my head and flung it far out, again and again. The trick was to bring it in, coiling it into the wooden tray gripped between your knees, at the right speed to keep it just clear of the bottom and hopefully passing under the nose of a large and hungry pike.

Suddenly this must have happened. I got a heavy bite and started hauling in for dear life. Out of the water came a great fish – about twelve kilos, I reckoned. It swung hammering into the side of my cliff, tore itself free and splashed back into the water. Hjördis sniffed.

A little while later (it couldn't have been the same fish,

surely) there was a heavy strike on the little boy's line.
He hauled in. The fish fought him, but he hung on
grim-faced. Then he began to give ground; he was being
pulled relentlessly down the beach. I shouted to him to let
go, but he wouldn't. Hjördis, up to her knees in the water
nearby, plunged over and got hold of the line with him.
But the fish must have got round a stone; the two of them
couldn't shift it.

Then Hjördis grabbed the bight of the line and hauled out
sideways, plunging deeper into the water. I knew she
couldn't swim, and bawled at her to drop it. She yelled back
something very rude to do with her behind. I was astounded.
Then, all at once, the line came free and together we hauled
the creature in, thrashing and snarling. It was the largest pike
I'd ever seen (16 kg by the fish-market man's spring balance
when he made his weekly visit). But the moment we got
home Hjördis was out again for her nets. She didn't even go
up to the house with her brother to tell them about their
monster pike. She really was a strange child.

It made me happy just to be with the Lindqvists. They all
had their jobs and I had mine, helping where I could –
cleaning and mending nets, lifting potatoes, sailing to market
with Ragnar and his böckling, and anything else that cropped
up – in return for as much fish, milk and potatoes as I
wanted.

Mrs Lindqvist and the elder daughter, Hilda, looked after
the chickens, four cows and a few sheep. But there was very
little grazing; so the cows had to be moved occasionally,
from one island to another by motor boat. The sheep could
manage better, but eventually they had sometimes to be
moved. Once in *Lilla Vän*; she could just take three of them.

I wondered what they did in winter time – that hard, dark
winter of the north, when the sun rose unwillingly, when it was
dusk all day and the sea and islands could be buried deep under
ice and snow. In a really hard winter the Gulfs of Finland and

Bothnia froze over completely. Shipping could only move through one or two channels kept open by ice-breakers. What did they do then, these hard-grafting, hurrying fisher people?

There must be work in the forests for some. And I'd heard about line-fishing through holes in the ice. But the children? Hjördis, what did she do? Would she be content with basket-making, weaving and a bit of carpentry? And the little boys? I thought of stubborn, stern-faced young Pelle hanging grimly onto his fishing line, refusing to be told by a stupid grown-up who didn't really know.

Thoughts like these came to me at night, when all was quiet except for the lapping of wavelets against my little boat, where I lay so peacefully and at ease, unconcerned about what next day would bring. It would bring the same as yesterday and the day before and the day before that. I was strangely untroubled by disquieting thoughts – of wars and politics or the wonders of science. They didn't really matter to us islanders; our lives were too full of living all day long.

But soon it was July, with 'Kvista löv' – collecting branches of beech, hazel and other deciduous trees or bushes for cattle fodder through the winter. In the islands there was very little grass, so they gathered green leaves instead. And there were parties for this too. For several weeks, a whole crowd of us would go from island to island cutting, stacking and transporting in our boats all the green stuff we could find (Plate 17) – including reeds from the more sheltered backwaters.

I was reminded of earlier days in London's Dockland – they seemed far off and long ago, though it was only two years since I had wandered with groups from dock to dock and ship to ship; losing a friend here, gaining a new one there – all different, with different backgrounds but a common problem. Except that here in Åland we had no immediate problems.

In the evenings we'd find a flat rock. Finland has large patches of ice-smoothed rock all over her forests and islands.

They make magnificent dance floors. All we needed was an accordion, sometimes a fiddle too, and plenty of 'spreet', and we could waltz the night away, with pine trees nodding in the night breeze around us. It was a wonderful life. Happy and hard-working, with people who seemed to be entirely without envy. I think in their heart of hearts they felt themselves superior, but were much too well-mannered to show it.

Although Elsa didn't dance – or said she didn't – she usually went along to the parties. There was as much chatting and singing (she couldn't sing either) as there was dancing. But she always seemed to be avoiding me, and I wondered why. Maybe it was my imagination, or she might have sensed that I'd want to monopolise her.

Then one morning, to my surprise, she came down to the boat-house and asked me to take her to a small uninhabited island west of Granö, where she said there were fish. She was wearing heavy corduroy trousers and a bulky rough woollen jersey, but she still had that ridiculous little knitted cap on the back of her head. She looked like a child, like Hjördis, shouting to me from along the jetty.

It took us nearly an hour to reach the island against a light south-westerly breeze. But as soon as we started fishing, we found that the effort hadn't been wasted. There were fish there alright, and before long we had as many pike and perch in our water butt as it would carry.

It was a heavenly summer's day, warm and gentle. The island was protected from the south by reefs, over which the sea ran in peacefully to lap against the shore. We made coffee in the lee of a boulder and I got out the brännvin to have with it. Elsa pulled off her jersey and opened the neck of a flimsy cotton shirt to let the wind blow through. Then she lay down on the hot rock, closing her eyes to face the sun. I did the same.

For a while we lay in silence, listening to the sea and thinking our thoughts. Mine were confused. What could

147

possibly have made Elsa come alone with me out here? She could have come in the motor-boat with one of the others, or on her own, by 'eker', for that matter.

'Winter's coming,' she said in Swedish at last, without opening her eyes. 'are you going away?'

'I don't know. Why?'

'Jan will be leaving soon to find a steamer. Ragnar's getting married when he's built a house on his girl's island. We'll need another man.'

This astonished me. It sounded like a direct invitation. And yet ... 'Would any man do?' I asked – a bit wryly, I suppose.

Elsa opened her eyes and sat up. The wind lifted one side of the shirt from her young breast. She looked enchanting.

'A man we can trust,' she said quietly.

'You think I would do?'

'Yes, but you might be difficult. That bothers me.'

'And if I promised not to be?'

'What are promises when the blood hammers in your ears?'

I sat up at that. 'What do you know about blood ... about men and their feelings?'

'I know my own'. Suddenly she swung round facing me. 'You think I'm cold. I'm not cold. My blood is warm like yours. May be warmer. But I won't let it rule me. I won't be anyone's woman, spending my life out here in the islands. I won't.' Her eyes were blazing now. No hint of that mocking smile. It was the longest speech I'd ever heard Elsa make. It came tumbling out in a sort of breathless shout. She moved closer impulsively, her eyes still alight, but not appealing, more demanding – a passionate demand for understanding. 'I must go before it's too late, Seligman (she'd always called me that, never Sam) ... before I'm caught. Do you understand?'

She turned away and there was silence for a while. Till I said quietly, and as calmly as I could:

'So you go and I stay ... is that the deal?'

She thought for a moment.

'Not at once,' then more insistently 'Not at once, Sam.'
She looked at me appealingly now, and I couldn't help
reaching for her hand. The blood was beginning to throb in
my throat and through my whole body. I could feel her
trembling as I put my arms round her; but she nestled closer,
warm and closer still. 'You will help me?' she whispered,
and I could see tears brimming in her eyes as I kissed them
one by one.

For a long time we clung together, until hazy cloud, high
up, began to steal across the sky. Elsa rose then, hitching up
her heavy trousers and pulling on her great jersey. The wind
had freshened from the south-west. We launched *Lilla Vän*
into the sea and put our things aboard, then made sail; and
thirty minutes later we came alongside the Lindqvists' jetty
on Granö.

We transferred our fish – three large pike, nearly a dozen
roach and one cod – from our water butt into one of the
floating fish-cages, where they would be kept alive until the
market motor-boat came to collect them.

Elsa watched for a moment, as they thrashed around
among the others, disturbing them. 'They'll settle down,' she
said, after a bit. And then, half-smiling ... 'and so should I,
maybe.' But I could tell that she was troubled.

21.

Autumn Days

For the rest of July, and on into August, we were all too busy to think of much else but getting the harvests in. On some of the islands there were meadows where we all helped with the hay-making. And 'Kvista löv' was a continuing occupation for young and old. Then there were apples to pick and potatoes to lift. And sheep had to be moved from island to island, wherever there were grassy clearings in the forest – too small for hay-making or cattle grazing, but ideal for flocks of a dozen or so sheep.

In late August, the woodlands were strewn with fungi – small and large, and some enormous – of every imaginable colour, from dowdy greys and mauves, through brown to olive green or tawny orange and dangerous-looking speckled crimson. Elsa knew the edible kinds. And one afternoon we went out with baskets and a few essentials, such as bread, cheese, fruit and a small bottle of brännvin; five or six kilos of fungi, to be dried for the winter, would be as good a return on half a day's work as any other.

It was cool in the forest, and dark; with pools of brilliance where shafts of sunlight pierced the canopy. And silent. Except for now and then the sudden scrabble of a red squirrel scampering up a tree, or leaping from branch to branch high up. Occasionally, too, the brief flutter of a bird, slipping secretly away through the undergrowth.

Fungi were everywhere, in clumps and clusters or on their own. Elsa pounced from one to the other, like a young kestrel; grabbing here, rejecting there.

'Look, *Karljohanssvamp*!' She held up a large shiny brown cap with a spongy pale underside ... 'favourites of Karl XIV Johan, Sweden's first French King. And there was another King (I can't remember his name) who loved *murklar* and was poisoned by his brother-in-law. *Murklar* – you call them *morels* – have to be boiled twice, throwing the water away each time, otherwise they can be killers.'

Under a fallen tree trunk, I found a colony of little light-brown trumpets which I recognised: 'How about these *chanterelles*?'

'I like these better.' Elsa had spotted a whole cluster of what she called *Tallblodriska* – large blood-red caps and gills growing close to the ground.

'And here – *Rynkad tofsskivling*'. Four yellowish round toadstools joined the others in her basket.

'And, oh look! *Svart Trumpetsvamp*. Best of all!' She pulled up one or two sinister-looking black trumpets ... 'But don't touch those white ones. Don't go near them. *Vit Flugsvamp*. They're deadly poisonous'. They looked it. Their slender white stems, white collars and dead white plate-like caps looked positively venomous.

And not far away, I came upon some brilliant red caps, with white gills and white collars round their stems. They looked dangerous too, but Elsa knew better: '*Smörsopp* are delicious when they're young' she put them in her basket and charged on, zigzagging here and there, like a young hound quartering the ground for the scent of game.

We went on like this for an hour or more. And there were berries too – blueberries and the scarlet cranberries. Elsa, in a flimsy summer dress, a satchel over one shoulder, blonde hair flying, seemed utterly tireless; until at last we both began to feel hungry.

In a clearing, where a stream chuckled among rocks, we lit a small fire of sticks, and Elsa took a pan out of her satchel to stew some of our 'catch'. We ate them with bread and cheese and a gulp or two of brännvin. Elsa was happy and, for once, relaxed.

I wanted to make the most of this – to keep the party cheerful ... 'You won't treat me like the poor king who loved morels, will you?'

'I'd rather take a hammer to you ... quicker ... and I will if you ask any more silly questions'. She leaned over and kissed me. I tried to grab her, but she escaped.

'And how about this fire? Is it allowed?'

'No. But I don't care, I feel fiery. Don't you?'

Before I could answer, she flung away, leaving me wondering. I could hear her crashing around as I cleared up and then followed her, in and out between the trees, over mossy mounds of ling and cranberry. When I caught up with her at last, she threw herself down on one of these mounds, laughing and exhausted, then turned to me with outstretched arms and shining eyes, head thrown back, her silky hair flooding softly over the moss.

I remember today the way she looked and the joy in her eyes. It was a moment of pure pleasure, which neither of us paused to think about; only to enjoy and go on enjoying into the warm and scented evening. After a while, a long and drowsy while, we got slowly to our feet and wandered homewards. For both of us, I think – for me at any rate – it had been a moment of enchantment, and nothing would ever be the same again.

By early September, with the ströming run abating, and fish moving further offshore, catches were growing smaller – often too small to be worth barrelling. So Ragnar was kept busier than ever at this smoke-house, curing batches of them. He'd hang the fish on rows of spikes, then light a fire and feed it with green juniper wood all day, till their skins were brown and shrivelled but their flesh still excellent to eat. Now too, there was other produce ready for the market – apples, beans, a few potatoes and once a sheep.

Lilla Vän was on the go every day, running in as much as

she could carry and bringing back supplies for the house and land. Sometimes Elsa came with me and we could talk. She had a remarkable understanding of many subjects, many values – in art and science, even literature, though it was a literature about which I knew nothing, hadn't even heard of, so I was the ignorant one there.

In any case, my most urgent thoughts were centred now on the future more than the past. I was twenty-four and the owner of a handy boat. I could easily make a living and more in summer time from fishing, helping on the land or as a carrier among the islands. In winter there would be work in the forest, where help was always welcome, and nets to mend, casks to make for next season's fishing, animals to look after and a hundred other tasks. And if I was careful, patient, tactful – my thoughts kept returning to this and wouldn't let it rest – Elsa might change her mind. She just might.

But Elsa didn't change her mind. She was kind to me now, at times even loving. Yet there were also times when, turning suddenly, I would catch her studying me with troubled eyes. She'd smile then, but uncertainly, and turn away to find some task or other to claim her attention, and the incident would pass, but not be forgotten by either of us.

She said no more about our forest interlude, nor about our morning on the island. But I knew she was worrying. Her fear of being tethered for ever to the life of a peasant kept nagging at her. And looking back now I realise how unfeeling I must have seemed; because, instead of offering to take her away to the Elysian fields she dreamed of, I thought and spoke of little else than building a life for both of us in Åland.

However, before the month was out, something happened that altered everything for both of us. A Swedish/American film crew arrived in Mariehamn to make a documentary on Åland and the Ålanders – or it may have been backing shots for some other film they were after. Anyway they came to

Granö, and from that moment everything changed. I don't know what it eventually led to, but several girls, including Elsa, got caught up in the project, and a few of the boys as well. The film people sent them here and there, paid them fantastic fees and generally took them out of circulation. So that was that.

It was a hard knock. And Elsa too may have had regrets at first. But in the end she must have got everything she longed for in Sweden or America. And as for me; with Elsa away there was so much work for the rest of us to get through – for father and mother Lindqvist, for Ragnar, Hilda and me, and of course Hjördis – that after a while the first agonies subsided. I began to find that life, even without Elsa, could be fulfilling.

But one day towards the end of September, Kalle-the-fishmarket brought a message. If he saw an Englishman from *Olivebank*, he'd been told he should say that two of Erikson's ships – *Olivebank* and *Viking* – would be signing on shortly. If Seligman wanted a berth on either of them, he must come to Mariehamn before the end of the week.

I sailed in two days later and signed on for *Olivebank*. The young man at the office looked at some report sheets he had by him and said 'Captain Mattson calls you keen and capable. Mr Frederikson says ... ' He looked up with a grin at my broken left eye-tooth ... 'he says you're hard to handle.' Then after a pause .... 'Could you handle an able seaman's job, d'you think?'

It was a great moment – one of the greatest of my life, of any young seaman's life. Of course I said 'Yes, sir', but inside me I was singing. It's difficult to explain, but the title 'Able Seaman' – the very ring of it – means more to a youngster going to sea than any other. He has become someone – someone to be reckoned with.

It was a Wednesday, I remember, and we weren't to join till the following Monday, so I got myself a bed at the sailor's home, and wandered off to look up a few friends. The younger Lindholm sister gave me coffee, the other one was at work and Eric was away. Jan, I knew, had already left to join his steamer in Helsingfors, but Ragnar came in with Kalle on the Friday, and we had a beer together.

Ragnar was a quiet unassuming sort of chap, three or four years older than Jan. He was always friendly to me, and I'd always helped him whenever I could.

'How will you develop your business?' I asked. 'You should have a boat of your own.'

'It would make things easier.'

'You'd better take mine. Will that help?'

'I really need a motor-boat to get round all the markets. But I'll look after yours till you come back.'

I'm sure he did. But I never saw either of them again. I don't know why. 'Gone shipmates' both, I suppose.

There was one last incident – last spasm one might call it – before Elsa became the happy memory she is today. The word went round that a dance was to be held on the Saturday evening in a Lemland Community Hall – Kirkvik, I think – and all my friends from round about would be going. I joined a party with a motor-boat which got us to the little town well before dark. It was autumn now, so that meant around 7.00 p.m.

The dance started at eight, by which time we had all been drinking for a couple of hours (everyone had a bottle with him). In fact, there'd been nothing much else to do for the past three days. So when we finally reached the dance hall we were in all sorts of moods – jolly, stupid, warlike, singing and generally in the party spirit.

Early on, there was a '*bruta armen*' contest (Indian wrestling, I think we call it) in which length of forearm matters most, and *Olivebank*'s new donkeyman, a jovial giant of a fellow with a great whooping guffaw of a laugh, had a longer forearm than the wolfish-looking Finn mainlander who'd taken him on.

Normally these battles are won and lost without too much show of bad temper. But in those days any argument between an Ålander and a mainland Finn was likely to end in violence. This one certainly did. They agreed to make it the best of three contest, but in fact they had four, and 'Donkey' won them all. This was more than the mainlander could take. At his fourth defeat, he sprang up, white to the lips, kicked the table aside and drew his knife. Luckily the police, who always attended these dances, were ready for this, so no blood was shed. But it was a tense moment.

Later, in fact it was close on midnight, a whole party of film people came rollicking in – Elsa and several other Ålanders among them. I was pretty far gone by then, but the sight of Elsa dancing, or rather lolloping around in the amorous clutches of one of the film people, must have set me off. I can just recollect barging over and saying something like: 'You can't dance, Elsa. Remember?' And then to the film chap, 'She doesn't dance. It's against her religion. Leave her alone, will you?'

There followed a fair amount of bashing and thumping and general fracas, in the middle of which I have a picture of Elsa's face – first scandalised, then appealing, then blazing with anger – like Hjördis with a big fish. Maybe Elsa had caught a fish herself. I didn't stay to find out; the whole thing was getting too much for me. I hurtled out into the street. The cold air hit me and sent me staggering, lurching away along a track leading out of the village. The forest closed in on either side. I didn't know where I was going and didn't care.

I felt that everything was lost. Everything I'd been living and planning for. The islands, Elsa, the good life, everything. Why had they left me? And why was I leaving them? Would I ever see any of them again? I staggered on and on and on into the forest.

The track grew narrower. The trees closed in. And all at once – I couldn't say just when – I felt friendly, helping arms under mine, and there was Lasse with two other chaps – Tefke and Harrinen, I found out later. They'd all just signed on *Olivebank* and heard rumours of a drunken Englishman floating around in Lemland somewhere. So they came to see what was going on. I was past caring, but we all got back to Mariehamn somehow, and next day (it must have been late afternoon) I woke up feeling weak and dazed but in surroundings I recognised – my bunk in *Olivebank*.

The psychological effect was instantaneous. After several weeks of intermittent but fairly powerful drinking, topped off by a monumental bender the night before, I was in a pitiful state of melancholy, ready to weep at just anything – the cat stroking its whiskers on the forecastle table, the wind in the rigging, loud laughter, anything. My bunk, my own home bunk, which I hadn't seen for months, gathered me in.

Inside my bunk, with the curtains drawn, was like inside a house. These were our own small houses, our homes, arranged in friendly pairs, one above the other, six down each side of the forecastle, like two-storey cottages round a market square. The curtains – neat, gaudy or serviceable, according to each man's taste – had been chosen with care (except by Koskinen, who had none at all). They gave a continental atmosphere to the narrow courtyard of wooden deck, round whose central table we ate, drank, fought, argued, dreamed and played the fool – at sea or in harbour, in every sort of weather and at all hours of the day and night.

Behind our curtains, when they were drawn, we lived our secret lives – became gentlemen of leisure, intellectuals, poets, fops, lovers – whatever each of us cared to fancy himself. The hubbub from the market square outside penetrated only to one's subconscious mind. We were cut off from it, secure and free for a while to sleep or read or dream in unassailable solitude.

I hunched round, like a dog settling into its basket. Everything was as I'd left it. The pictures on the bulkhead from a Swedish magazine beamed, beckoned or bewitched according to their kind. On the shelves at the foot were all my possessions – an emu's egg, half a dozen Albatross Editions (there were no Pans or Penguins in those days), a sail palm and needle, innumerable shells, a half-finished shoe made of ropeyarn sennet, a bottle of glue, one of ink, some soap and two toothbrushes in a home-made rack tacked to the woodwork, a photograph of Sheila and her friend Pen on a hillside behind Cadgwith. In an alcove above my head, a stump of candle which guttered contentedly when I lit it.

On the bench beside my bunk lay my seabag unopened. Lasse must have brought it from the sailor's home. Lasse was a marvel. How had he managed to get me here, stowed away and for the moment safe? And what price now, this fine young able seaman, this man to be reckoned with? In Scandinavia in those days, a good booze-up from time to time didn't bother anyone – it was the done thing. But in a ship at sea, or about to sail ... well, thank God for Lasse anyway. My seabag would have to wait, however, I was too weak and tired just then to do anything about it. Instead I turned over again and went to sleep.

The next thing I became conscious of was a thump against the ship's side, followed by shouting and the stamping of feet. I lurched out on deck to find that the tug Johanna had put a hawser aboard, and we were already moving down harbour with loosed sails ready for sea. Why I hadn't been called, I didn't know. Maybe we had new mates who hadn't mustered the crew yet, and the boys just let me lie in.

I was sober now, but still weak as a chicken. I remember standing alone out on deck as we turned, increasing speed down the western channel. I also remember tears of hopeless self-pity and exhaustion streaming down my face as we passed the islands one by one and the scent of pines grew fainter as the fjord widened towards the open sea.

Three whistles ... 'Fore and main upper topsails! ... Main staysail!..' The mates came clattering down the poopladders to join in the trample of running feet, followed by thud upon thud as sheet, brace and halyard coils were snatched from their pins and flung down on deck. *Olivebank* began to lift to a low swell running in against her. Instinctively I tailed on with the crowd on the fore topsail halyards.

'Hey, Sam! ... You not dead then?' Harrinen's loud and laughing voice came like a splash of cold water, reviving and cheering. 'Here ... come ... ' He gave me a great thump on the shoulder, and I found I could grin back at him as he made room for me on the rope. It was like coming to life from a deep and troubled sleep – a new life with new shipmates.

'Heja-ho! Heja-ho.' The yards rose creaking up the masts. Their sails filled. The tug was cast off and fell away to port. Shouting, stamping, rush and bustle, as sail after sail was set and the ship gathered way. Outward bound! Outward bound again for another year at sea, maybe more.

Part V
Final Voyages

22.

North About

There wasn't much wind in the Baltic that autumn, and what there was of it was contrary. We worked our way down to Oscarshamn on the Swedish coast, where we spent nearly a week in dry dock. Then on to Copenhagen, where we lay for another two days at anchor, provisioning ship. And then, at last, a fine fair wind up the Kattegat to the Skaw.

We had two new officers – Captain Lindvall and the Mate, Fågelström, a tough and exceptionally efficient man who knew his own mind and made sure that others knew it too. Last trip's 3rd Mate, Blomqvist, a kindly and rather easy-going fellow by contrast, had been promoted to 2nd Mate. The carpenter, that iron-fisted block of muscle, who'd failed to conquer the heart of a fifteen-foot shark, but was otherwise jovial and a friend to all, had now been appointed 3rd Mate. He made sure at once – he had to – that the dear old days were gone forever; in future we'd jump to it or, as far as he was concerned, jump overboard.

Everyone else, except Lasse and I and the two German apprentices (Hoffman had gone home) were new to the ship. There was a new sailmaker – brother of Blomqvist, the second mate, and a giant of a man like the new donkeyman. Also a new carpenter who, by contrast, was small and slight and rather nervy. Then there were eight jungmän – five of them from the same small town on an island off the West coast of Finland. These five did everything together whenever they could, and we thought of them together – Nab, Back, Brink, Grahn and Fågelklo from Replot; it made a cheery jingle, which we liked repeating.

This was the new skipper's first command, and we wondered how he'd make out. We weren't kept long in doubt. The wind freshened from the east and sent us flying out into the North Sea, at which point every captain of a southbound sailing vessel had to make a difficult choice – whether to take the shorter, more direct (but also more crowded and restricted) route through the English Channel, or the longer, harder way, with more sea room, north of Scotland – maybe north of Orkney and Shetland too, and out through the Faeroes Passage.

Easterly and north-easterly winds, with low pressure over France, can hold sometimes for weeks in spring and autumn, and the strong east wind that was driving us along just now might have tempted many skippers to try the southern route. It was close on sunset. Captain Lindvall looked at the glass, then at the sky and sails.* 'We'll go north about,' he said. 'Steer north-west by west.' Then to the second mate: 'Check all the hatches and the ballast. It's going to blow.'

We turned to the new course, and almost at once the wind began to veer. By next morning it was blowing half a gale from south – a dead head-wind for any vessel making for the Straits of Dover. Before we reached Shetland that evening, there was a full gale from south-west, and *Olive-bank* was down to topsails and foresail, pounding into high seas with a long Atlantic swell running through them.

It wasn't long before the foresail had to come in, and the fore and mizzen upper topsails. It was a hard fight, especially for the new hands. None of the new jungmän had been in sail before; one or two had never been to sea. The older ones helped them all they could, but the constant plunging and heaving and rolling of the ship, this way and

---

* As far as I know, there were no broadcast weather reports in those days, and anyway we had no radio aboard.

that, in violent cross seas, made it a battle for all of us. A squall with sleet hit us soon after dark, and the temperature dropped sharply. Ten of us went aloft to furl the main upper topsail. We fought with it for nearly an hour (Plate 19). When we came down, our fingers were numb and our eyes so red and caked with salt that for quite a while I was seeing double, as though drunk.

The gale continued, but with the passing of that squall, the wind veered again, and was now blowing from due west out of a clearing sky. It was bitterly cold, but we daren't put on gloves in case there came a sudden call – something carried away or needing to be secured. Spray flew in clouds across the ship from every wave-top. The watch sheltered where they could in odd corners; the potato locker forward was a favourite haunt. The watch below got what rest they could in the forecastle, lying on the deck or benches with their oilskins on. Many slept. Here's how I described it in the duplicate exercise book my mother gave me to take to sea:

'The men lurch wearily over the storm-step into the forecastle and stand blinking for a moment in the light of the oil lamp swinging in wide asymmetrical curves from the deckhead, like a tethered animal trying to dodge a rain of unseen blows. It's a wild night. The ship groans and heaves and lies over to the assault of the wind and mountainous cross seas. There's no rest for her, nor for anyone in her.

'Most of the watch have thrown themselves down fully clothed on the deck to catch a few hours sleep before being called out again at a quarter to four. Glistening bundles of oilskin and warm clothing, they roll gently from side to side with the working of the ship. They look lifeless. An occasional whimper comes out of young Kalle, as though from a soul in torment, sharing the agony of the ship. But he's sound asleep; has been almost from the moment his head touched the deck (wearing the fur cap his mother brought aboard the day we sailed).

'I can't sleep myself, so I'm sitting wedged between the fresh water tank and the side of my bunk to get what rest I can. Koskinen and two of the new hands – youngsters from the West Coast who speak no Finnish – are sitting at the forecastle table. Between them is an enamel dish containing lumps of cold salt beef and a few broken pieces of biscuit. Koskinen is holding forth as usual. He always does at the beginning of a voyage, especially to the new hands. His strange guttural mixture of broken English and equally broken Swedish rumbles on, remorseless and demanding, like the storm outside.

'"No word from her, plotty – only pointing to de Rolls Royce and looking .. Den, after me, she getting inside, and we driving and driving miles in de country. She not speaking von vord ... Plotty Hell, I am getting frightened from dis pewtiful devil that is sitting as a ghost near me on de seat. And de chauffeur and footman, as stuffed animals in front, not asking any tings. Devils and Hell, I am scared.

'"By and by ve coming in a pewtiful park, and after some kilometres a great house, like palace, vere ve are stopping. She getting out and calling me "Come!", den going up many great steps. De door opening himself. I following inside vere is not too much light; but ven ve are climbing in de stairs I am seeing furnishings, pictures and carpets. Plotty! Vort millions!

'"After ve are coming to de boudoir and going inside, she locking de door. Plotty, I am saying, vat now? But she, cold like ice, taking quickly off her clothes and pointing me to also do it. And ven I am seeing her naken and pewtiful before me, I am quickly understanding also, my vord, I tell you ... "

'Koskinen laughs, a great roaring laugh, and looks from one youngster to the other and back. They gape at him, one holding a biscuit half way to his mouth. There are crumbs on his lower lip, but he's too enthralled to notice and brush them off. Koskinen goes on: 'You know vat she is vanting?'

he asks dramatically. 'Devils and Satan, I vill tell you. She going to von locker and taking out dog vip. "Strook me" she crying out.

'"I am shaking. Plotty! Vat can I do? She screaming all de time "Strook me, you plotty boggers Finn. Strook me till it is plot coming!" And ven I am only standing like big pig, she quickly tearing de vip over my face ... von ... two ... tree times. Devils and Perkele, but I am mad now, gripping in my hands de vip and at vonce smashing her down. Den I strook and I strook, and I am roaring like mad, and she laughing and skreeking on de ground. I tell you. Plotty boggers Satan! I tell you!"

'Lars – tall, sinewy, taciturn – heaves himself up from the cross-bench aft, on which he was lolling, and lurches forward to the water tank. He draws a mug of water and drinks with deliberation. His face has an austere and brooding look. He takes no notice of Koskinen, now leaning over the table and glaring with mad intensity at the boy nearest to him. We have all heard that story about the dog whip, and others like it. Everyone who has been any time at sea has heard them. They come from the great unwritten anthology of the Hamburg, Rotterdam, Antwerp and Liverpool waterfronts.

'They are all very much alike, and one of their central figures is invariably a beautiful, aristocratic and fabulously wealthy woman, who demands the muscular attentions of sailors. The climax is always set amid luxurious surroundings. Costly curtains and carpets abound (curtains and carpets always figure prominently in sailors' dreams). Obsequious flunkeys bring in rich foods and drink. These have been, for a century or more, the accepted fairy tales of the seafaring fraternity; as genuine, and in some ways as poignant, as 'Hansel and Gretel' with its house in the forest made of good things to eat.

'When he has finished drinking at the water tank. Lars stands for a moment looking down with a passing and untroubled interest at the group round the table; then he lurches aft again, inscrutable and indifferent. He slumps down on the bench beside his bunk on the port side and is soon asleep.

'But I stay awake. The heavy labouring of the ship, and the intermittent crash of big seas against the steel plates of her hull jar the nerves. One grows resentful at this perpetual bullying of a valued friend.

'Nevertheless, to pass the time, I am listening to Koskinen and the two boys. The story will not interest me much, unless Koskinen has hit on some new and unusual slant. But Koskinen himself and the other two do interest me. They are my shipmates and will be my friends; after Lars, the closest friends I'll have for the best part of a year. Koskinen himself I have known for more than a year, the two boys for about ten days, yet they people my world equally and, with others like them, entirely. There is no world anyway, for any of us, beyond this ship and the tormented disc of the sea on which she swims.'

Such was the first gale of our second voyage in *Olivebank*. It was a voyage like any other, with the same sort of hopes and disappointments, triumphs and failures. And yet it was different. For me it was very different. As soon as the Trade Winds found us, and more settled weather could be relied on, Lasse and I were taken out of our watches and put on day work. We and another A.B., Vihersalo, were given a mast and rigging each. I got the foremast, and every day after breakfast I'd disappear aloft with my bag of tools, spunyarn, sail twine, seizing wire and the like, to overhaul, repair, grease, paint or serve anything and everything, from shackles, blocks, buntlines, clewlines and rovings to backstays, shrouds, ratlines, batons, footropes, stirrups and everything appertaining to all or any of them.

It was steady, satisfying work away from all the fuss and bother of life around the decks. We answered no whistles, except three whistles to call all hands; but this seldom, if ever, happened in Trade Wind weather. We were alone and happy, looking up at great castles of white canvas, stiff with wind, or down at a long slim hull forging powerfully ahead through glittering seas (Plate 20), the warm wind pouring over and around us.

On Saturday afternoons and Sundays we were free. And it was then that I started to write a weekly piece in my mother's duplicate books. 'You'll get pictures' she had said, 'true pictures before they fade'.

And time was a friend. There was a complete lack of urgency in everything we did. There was always time enough to do things properly, to concentrate first and always on getting it right. Time also to think, and think deeply. In the evenings, we daymen and some of the watch below would lay our mattresses on the main hatch and talk and doze, and talk and doze and talk, till the stars began to pale and day was at hand.

23.

Kangaroo Hunt

On January 25th, 1934, *Olivebank* reached Port Lincoln, 111 days out from Copenhagen, and we were delighted to hear, on arrival, that we would be loading at Port Lincoln itself. There'd be no sweating up the Gulf under sail to one of the other ports. And Port Lincoln was said to be livelier and more interesting than any of the others.

There followed the usual shuffling in and out, under sail mostly, between the inner and outer anchorages and the jetty. The difficulty was that we couldn't discharge all our ballast until we had a bit of cargo aboard to take its place and ensure stability. So two separate shifts had to be made, and there wasn't always a tug available, or it was too costly, or the wind was too strong or from the wrong direction.

In all, the de-ballasting operation took the best part of two weeks. Finally, the skipper wound it up with one of the most spectacular feats of seamanship most of us had ever seen. It might well have ended in disaster, but was in fact triumphantly successful. With a light easterly breeze behind him, Captain Lindvall sailed his ship under topsails, staysails and spanker, straight at the wooden jetty at about four knots. One ship's length from it, when a rending, splintering crash looked inevitable, he let go his starboard anchor and snubbed her round on it, so that she literally fell alongside – gently and without any trouble – sails set and all (Plate 21). It was an impressive performance.

We were now free at last to come and go ashore as we pleased and whenever we felt like it. We certainly made the most of this, and so did the people of Port Lincoln. Every evening, the long wooden jetty at which we lay became a promenade. Girls arm-in-arm, in groups and pairs, elderly couples, whole families, groups of children and one or two solitary strollers sauntered up and down, exchanging greetings or stopping to chat. Many paused to stare aboard, or aloft at the masts and yards, looking unaccustomedly tidy with their harbour-stowed sails. Some came up the gangway and wandered about our decks, looking in at each of the deckhouses in turn with friendly greetings. *Olivebank* had added an attractive seaside terrace to the scant amenities of a small bush town.

Even some of the lumpers who'd been loading wheat bags during the day came down in the evening to chat with us on board or on the jetty. And almost every day some of us were asked home for an Australian tea, with chops or kippers (sometimes both), eggs and bacon, mugs of tea and afterwards beer, at home or in the pub.

But the cargo came aboard even more slowly than at Port Victoria the year before. Parcels of twenty or thirty bags from inland farms would arrive alongside from time to time, delivered by horse-drawn waggon, sometimes only one waggon a day. We needed around fifty-four thousand bags for a full cargo, so it looked as though we were in for a long stay.

People began to get restive and irritated over trifles. Imagined injustices were raked up from the past. One in particular: when ballast was being discharged it had also been necessary to send down sails to preserve them against sand and grit in the desert winds. But it hadn't been practical to do both jobs together, so the sails were reserved for one Saturday afternoon and Sunday morning.

This had annoyed us mildly at the time, though out in the roadstead, unable to get ashore, it really hadn't been much of a hardship. Now, however, the monstrous injustice of it, blown up to majestic proportions by that amiable young firebrand,

Kalle Häkkinen, got everybody going. We must go aft in a body! Insist on our rights! Down tools, boys! Not another stroke till we get our overtime!

So it was decided. And more to help keep the peace than for any other reason, I agreed to act as spokesman – provided that we were a proper deputation of four or five, and not the baying mob that Kalle favoured. So I got my first (and only) taste of Trades Union bossery, and discovered at once that I was never going to become a Nye Bevan or a Jack Jones. In the end all we got was a bit of overtime for working ballast, but nothing for sending down the sails.

Worse still, for the next two Sundays we were made to scrub decks from 7.00 to 8.00 a.m. – a practice on which Captains apparently had the right to insist under Finnish maritime law.

Kalle was furious – or said he was, though he was still grinning broadly as he outlined what should have happened: 'We should have broken the place up, all of us! We should have cut his head off and made him eat it! We should have ... ' But nobody took Kalle very seriously, and most were content to have made a point and a bit of overtime to spend ashore in the evenings.

Then something happened which took our minds off everything else. It was on the second Friday alongside that Frank Bolger, one of the lumpers, came into the forecastle at dinner time and sat himself down on the sea chest at the end of the table. 'I got the loan of a waggon,' he said. 'Any of you jokers want to come out in the country tomorrow? We'll take the dogs and see if there's any 'roos about. We'll be away all night.'

Almost everyone at the table jumped at the offer; and the donkeyman, who'd dropped in for a yarn, wanted to come too. It was astonishing to me that these Scandinavians, from a land of lakes and forests, wanted to trek out under a burning sun into the desert which we all knew extended for more than a thousand miles to the North and West of Port Lincoln.

But they did, and next morning fifteen of us, with Frank and his two greyhounds, piled onto a two-horse waggon, sitting on boxes or on the open flat with legs dangling over the edge all round. The Finns and Frank got on wonderfully together. In a way, it seemed as though, in spite of language difficulties, they understood each other better than I understood any of them. And again I was surprised.

It was late February and blistering hot. From the brow of the first low hill overlooking the bay we could see for miles across a burnt and rolling plain dotted with trees. Ringed and dead, everyone of them. Some fallen. They littered the landscape, giving it a strangely ancient as well as barren appearance. It was difficult to believe that these were the famous wheatlands of the Spencer gulf. They stretched as far as we could see, to right and left and way ahead of us. By noon it was still the same, except that now there was a seemingly limitless expanse of parched and dusty plain behind us too.

The sun blazed down. Now there was wheat on either side of the track, stretching again as far as we could see. Yet there was still no sign of life, except now and then a pale green bloom – a sort of fuzz over the top of the wheat – rising and falling, appearing and disappearing. We thought at first that it must be a swarm of locusts; but it wasn't, it was birds – budgerigars (shell parrots they call them) in twittering flocks of two or three thousand together, floating and settling across the wheat.

Once or twice we saw iguanas – slow, ugly brutes – and occasionally rabbits. Till, after another ten miles we topped a second rise and came on the most surprising spectacle of all – a large green tree, alone in the desert, and apparently smothered in blossom. It looked like Magnolia, or perhaps a giant pink and white orchid entwined in the branches. But as we approached, it suddenly exploded – there's no other word for it – the flowers burst into the air and became a cloud of screaming cockatoos. The scene seemed to epitomise South Australia – a land, they say, where the flowers have no scent and the birds no song. The tree, when we reached it, turned out to be a mulberry in full fruit, with near it the ruins of a farm and a well filled with stones. We spent a happy twenty minutes there, gorging ourselves on fruit the cockatoos hadn't had time to guzzle.

After a while we drove on and soon the ground began to rise. The wheat fields disappeared, giving way to stony hills cut up by ravines. Presently we stopped, and Frank slipped his dogs. 'Just the place for a 'roo,' he said, 'on the edge of the wheat.'

Then we saw them – a row of inquisitive heads peering at us over the skyline of a nearby hillock. There must have been seven or eight of them, and after one startled look at us they were off, scattering in all directions, bounding over rocks, trees, bushes and ravines as though they hardly existed. The dogs streaked after them, yelping hysterically.

Some got away. One even doubled back and cleared a dried-up watercourse close by with a leap of thirty feet or more. But two were less fortunate; the dogs pulled them down and tore their throats out. It was a sickening performance, yet somehow in tune with the hard, harsh life of the land.

'They have to be kept down,' said Frank. 'They destroy whole acres of wheat, and no fence is high enough to keep 'em out.' But of course the Finns didn't need such explanations. They also came from a hard land; some of them from the far north, almost as far as the tundra of Lapland. I began to understand the affinity between Frank and them.

We were now in sheep country, or rather land which had supported sheep before the wells failed. It looked an utter wilderness, and we saw no more wild life except a covey of emus, looking for all the world like animated pin-cushions, and every bit as stupid. They all made for the same gap in a wire fence close to the road and landed in a kicking, squabbling heap on the other side.

That night we camped in the bush round an enormous fire, made by simply hauling three or four dead trees together, adding some branches to fill in the gaps and dried grass for tinder. A single match set it roaring, and when it had died down a little, we roasted kangaroo steaks on the ends of long pointed sticks. Afterwards we lay in a wide circle round the embers while the billy boiled for tea; and beside it another pot in which kangaroo tail chops simmered for breakfast. We sang songs and listened to tales of the bush, which Frank told in his slow, unemotional drawl. He told us of giant spiky lizards; of carpet snakes and the aborigines who ate them; of gold and drought and monster cattle drives to find water. And the Finns capped his yarns with folk tales from the North.

We dragged one or two more trees onto the fire, and when it died down again we gathered closer, wrapped in coats and blankets. But I doubt if anyone slept much. I didn't. I think it was the silence out there – the utter absence of sound or movement which belongs neither to the sea, nor to forests, but only to desert places. Some time during the night, I remember, we heard barking and the long drawn howl of a dingo. But apart from that the silence persisted. Even after the sun had risen, there was no quickening to life at dawn in this naked land, so that I began to wonder how men could love it as they did, as Frank undoubtedly did. And even some of my Finnish shipmates. They seemed enchanted by it, ready even to jump ship and try their luck there. Perhaps it did indeed remind some of them of their native Lapland: the same bare and limitless spaces, the same hostility, the same passionate antiquity.

And the same invincibility. Even the Aussies, courageous, unquenchable folk though they were, would point almost with pride to the vast areas of their backlands which still defied cultivation – areas in which the kookaburra, the desert kingfisher, with his maniac laugh, was one of the few creatures who seemed completely at home. Perhaps, too, it was this same pride in their country's invincibility by man which had prompted them to make the kookaburra (the laughing jackass they called him) one of their national emblems.

24.

Stranger at Noon

Loading continued at the same slow pace. We began to grow into the place, become part of Port Lincoln itself. We were regulars now at one or two of the boozers, and some of the boys even got themselves steady girlfriends.

Koskinen was different. He didn't dislike women. Far from it. But hard liquor was his main preoccupation. He hadn't many friends ashore, however, because although he was a warm-hearted and often humorous fellow, when he got drunk he was a terror. His vanity about his appearance was, in a way, endearing, because it was flaunted with so much gusto. And women loved him, even though he treated them abominably.

Then there was Jeff. In the middle of a noisy argument round the forecastle table, after the midday meal one day, I happened to look up and there he was, in the doorway – short and scraggy, with a gaunt, hungry-looking face and sandy hair, in khaki shirt and shorts, bare legs and brown gym-shoes – staring at us.

We stared back, and for a moment no one spoke. Then he went to the head of the table, where plates and dishes had been roughly stacked beside a bucket of warm water, and began to do the washing-up. The lad nearest to him who should have been doing it, made some remark which I didn't catch; and someone called from the other end of the table:

'What's your name?'

'Jeff.'

'Jeff what?'

'That's right ... Jeff What.'

We never discovered his full name. He had no papers, and wouldn't have been able to read them if he'd had any. But he was English, that much he admitted to. He'd been on the bum in Australia for the past five years, trapping rabbits, doing odd jobs, living for months in the out-back. He'd drifted into Port Lincoln a few days ago, and if he liked it he'd stick around for a bit.

He did like it, or liked *Olivebank* anyway. And the Finns quite liked him. He was unobtrusive and obliging, with occasional flashes of dry humour, and he did the washing-up which we all hated. In a host of other ways too, he made himself useful – mending clothes, running errands, fetching our food from the galley, sweeping out the forecastle; soon he'd become a part of the scenery, with the spare bunk to sleep in whenever he wanted it.

As for me, I have to confess that the man fascinated me – his reserve, his quick perception and grasp of any situation, of peoples' moods, their strengths and weaknesses, like an animal intent on survival in unfamiliar surroundings.

There was also something mysterious about him that was difficult to fathom – something ancient, almost primaeval about his way of life – the age-old aboriginal life of Australia. Jeff had spent the best part of two years with an Abo family on long, slow wanderings in the desert; through the Gawler hills and the lakes and marshland further north; hunting, fishing, finding berries, roots and insects; digging for water in sandy gullies. His eyes, except that they were brilliant blue, held the same permanently watchful expression that you see in primitive people; and he had a habit of going through doors sideways, as though trying to keep a look-out in front and behind at the same time.

Once, for a short spell after the First World War, Jeff had been in the British Army in Germany, though how he'd passed any education tests was difficult to understand: he could hardly read, and wrote with difficulty. There were also surprising gaps in his general knowledge: he couldn't for example, conceive the Earth as round; the idea meant nothing to him. For Jeff all countries lay further away or nearer, on a broad, flat ribbon of land and sea stretching to infinity in both directions – Germany one way, Australia the other, with France, Britain and America somewhere in between ... I doubt if he'd ever thought about any other countries.

And yet he was shrewd. Jeff had a depth of understanding that surprised even me. He was also religious. His religion was stability – stability and security. It was a man's duty, he considered, to look after himself before everything. 'Watching points', he called it. A man ought to use every atom of guile and cunning he possessed to achieve stability and security, and he should know how to 'work the oracle' to that end. A good watcher of points and worker of the oracle was a boon to society. All others were a nuisance.

From my duplicate book:
I wake to find Jeff sitting on the bench beside my bunk, staring anxiously into my face and shaking my shoulder gently.

'I thought you was dead', he says, looking disappointed. 'But as you ain't ... ' he points to a plate of rapidly congealing mutton, cabbage and potatoes on the forecastle table and makes way for me to get out of the bunk.

I was night-watchman last night. Now its nearly three in the afternoon, and I'm on again tonight. Except for the two of us the forecastle is empty. Shafts of sunlight from the skylight overhead form bright squares on table and bulkhead, moving gently as *Olivebank* rocks a little at her moorings. Flies are everywhere, describing intricate patterns in the air or dog-fighting delicately about the food, the oil lamp hanging over the table and our faces.

'D'you want this?' Jeff is holding out an Adelaide newspaper. I glance at the front page, still eating. There's something about a defensive Balkan pact, which Hungary has boycotted. Last week it was Dollfuss banning the Nazi Party in Austria. And the day after we arrived in Port Lincoln, Hitler had signed a ten-year non-aggression pact with Poland. It all sounded very tiresome and boring. Thank God we'd soon be at sea and away from it all.

'What do you think about all this?' I ask Jeff, pointing to the page.

'Never troubled to look at it.' It's an accepted convention that Jeff doesn't trouble about the press. In fact, though, he can't read.

'The Germans'll soon be in Vienna.'

'Arr.'

When I've finished eating, I go back to my bunk and drag out go-ashore trousers from under my mattress, and my last clean shirt from the suitcase under my bunk.

'You better give me that later on,' Jeff says.

'I can wash it myself when we get up into the Trades.'

'Not like Clara can.'

Clara, we understand, is a widow living over the other side of town, who will wash and iron shirts for a few shillings, when she has time. 'Not fer anyone, she won't ... I 'elped 'er out once. Now she 'elps me, see?' Jeff wants us to be quite clear about this.

Some of the lads find it less trouble to give a shirt to Jeff occasionally than wash it themselves. In harbour, loading cargo, there aren't many drying places where a wet shirt won't get covered in dust. One or two have even tried to find out where Clara lives, but Jeff's always ready for that one. 'Tryin' ter cut me out, are yer? Think I'm soft, or somethin'?'

As Jeff and I approach the gangway to go ashore, we are conscious of raised voices in the half-deck aft. Leimbach, in his smart uniform is standing by the rail, apparently oblivious to the commotion.

'Why ain't you in Vienna, mate?' Jeff asks, hoping to get a rise out of him. He likes to show us that he's a forecastle man, not a half-deck toady.

Leimbach looks round. 'Theoretically' he says gravely 'I *am* in Vienna, or soon will be.' His eyes are smiling. He loves being clever in English.

The rumpus in the half-deck seems to be growing. I'm interested. 'What's going on in there?'

'Scheibel has embarked upon the difficult task of persuading some of our Finnish shipmates that the New Order will solve all the world's problems.'

'D'you believe that?'

'I believe in Germany.'

'And Hitler?'

'I come from the Rhineland.' Leimbach is smiling again, because he knows that I won't be able to work out whether that means yes or no. 'Scheibel is a Sudeten', he adds genially, to confuse things further.

Jeff and I move off along the jetty. Just before we reach the shore end, on our way to the pub, Scheibel and Leimbach overtake us, marching along with a martial swing. They are smartly turned out in their German merchant service uniforms. In a car on shore, two girls from one of the many German families in South Australia are waiting to greet them. The boys salute together, then embrace the girls with gusto and at some length.

Jeff isn't a drinker. After a lager and half a pint of shandy he leaves me. When I get back to the ship later, the evening promenade of townspeople is in full swing. One or two of our Finns sit talking to friends or stroll arm-in-arm with girls along the jetty. The Captain, in a white shirt, duck trousers and a uniform cap, is leaning with his hands on the poop rail, chatting to the bank manager on the jetty.

By the time I have changed, and placed lighted hurricane lamps at both ends of the gangway, the sun has set.

Soon it grows dark. The people on the jetty drift away. The captain and the bank manager stroll after them.

The mates have got girls down in the saloon. Their distant giggles invade the stillness, like the rustle of autumn leaves in random eddies of the wind. After a while these also cease, and silence descends upon the ship.

The night is quite still now, the breeze has fallen away to nothing, and with the turn of the tide the swell has subsided, leaving the ship motionless against the jetty. The darkness pressing down on her swarms with stars. One can imagine them very close above the mast-heads – a countless company of celestial Jeffs, peering down on us with pity and surprise, watching attentively – watching points.

How I envy Jeff his detachment, his single-mindedness, his positive genius for self-preservation and, above all, his complete escape from the turmoil and ever-growing pace of life I found overpowering at home in England.

Here in South Australia, in the out-back – the yellow desert, reeking hot and littered with the skeletons of trees – here it's different. South Australia to me is a land of miracles, where beauty flowers in the wilderness in surprising ways. And further west, beyond the Nullabor – gold! The lure of it is always there; not of the gold itself so much, as of the patient search for it in lonely places.

Later

In the forecastle Jeff stands over a wooden bucket full of knives and forks and dirty plates, which he is washing and drying with care. Behind him, in the shadows, Koskinen is lurching about, singing in a raucous mumbling way, with occasional loud shouts. He is very drunk. It has been one of his special nights, when he goes off into the bush on his own with a bottle. He has his knife out and is making ferocious feints at Jeff's unconscious back in time with his singing. Whenever he forgets the words, which is most of the time, he fills in with 'Blaady bastard Englishmen' or some such observation of a more or less obscene or offensive nature.

Jeff takes no notice. He is drying the knives deliberately and arranging them in a flower-like pattern in the middle of the scrubbed deal table.

'Where you bin?' he asks me sternly. Then ...

'You'll get in trouble with that Liz.'

'Who told you I was with Liz?'

'Liz, Liz ... blaady, blaady, Ranan Järvinen' chants Koskinen in the background.

'I know you was' says Jeff 'and I also know things you maybe don't ... Abaht Liz.'

I'm in no mood to listen to Jeff's ideas about Liz. She's a lively little person who has brightened my life for a while, and I shall miss her. But Koskinen is drooling on – about blaady Englishmen, about fighting Finns, about Jeff, about Liz.

'Women!' says Jeff, with enormous scorn. Then he goes to the water tank and draws a mugful. He hands it to Koskinen. 'Here ... ' he says. Koskinen takes it clumsily, without looking. Jeff turns back to his washing up. 'No savvy, neither of you ... no stability.'

When he has finished he takes up the bucket to empty it over the side. Koskinen is now between him and the door, mouthing and raving, his knife still carving the air in front of him. Jeff stands quite still, watching him carefully. All at once he gives him a quick shove in the chest that catches him off balance and sends him staggering back into his corner muttering 'blaady ... blaady ... blaady'.

During the fifteen seconds or so that Jeff is out on deck, Koskinen collects himself and comes weaving forward again. Jeff comes back, glances at him sharply, then stoops to put the bucket under the table.

As he does so, Koskinen lurches towards him. Jeff, still bending down, lifts one leg and kicks straight out behind him. The heel of his shoe catches Koskinen a glancing blow on the chin. He crumples and falls with a crash.

Jeff straightens up and looks down at him. 'Time 'e flopped aht, an' all,' he observes impassively.

'Get him into his bunk, shall we?'

'Naah. Leave 'im.' Jeff turns down the oil lamp and makes for the door. 'Drunks never come to no 'arm'. He pauses with one foot on the storm step, looking warily out into the darkness, as though weighing his chances of reaching the next bright haven (the Y.M.C.A. hut, where he sometimes lodges) unmolested ... 'so long as they keep off the women', he adds darkly, then takes a quick bird-like hop out on deck, slips sideways into the shadows and disappears.

That is the whole of Jeff's life ... watching carefully, weighing his chances, acting and slipping away. I wonder whether Koskinen will remember and bear a grudge in the morning. Probably not, or Jeff would have known it and acted differently. Yes, Jeff would have known.

25.

Falmouth for Orders

Towards the end of February, *Olivebank* had nearly a full cargo aboard. The mate was keeping a watchful eye on her load line and especially on her trim. If she was too much by the head, she'd be a pig to steer; if by the stern, there was always a danger of 'pooping' in a high following sea.

It was the practice, when loading grain in bags, to open a few from time to time and bleed them of their contents; the loose grain was supposed to sink into the cracks between bags and help to bind the cargo together. But the trouble was that if the bleeding was uneven throughout the length of the ship, this could affect her trim. So there was a continuing four-cornered battle between the three gangs of lumpers and the mates. Each gang wanted to get as many bags as possible, full or bled, into its hold (more bags, more money), while the mates were equally concerned about seaworthiness in the Southern Ocean.

In those days there were no cranes on the jetty at Port Lincoln. Ships had to use their own gear – gin-blocks slung from the rigging, with the donkey boiler to power winch drums from which the guys and falls were worked. It was a slow business; but since the cargo came in slowly too, this didn't much matter.

What did matter – as before, when we discharged the ballast – was that the donkey boiler and winch drums couldn't be used for sending sails aloft at the same time as bringing bags of wheat aboard. So it wasn't until February 26th, when the last of the cargo had been stowed, that we were able to start bending on sails. This took the best part of two days. Then we needed more coal for the galley, and a reserve supply for the donkey boiler, so that it could be used for working the anchor and for changing sails in the tropics.

By 10.00 a.m. on February 28th we were ready for sea. And it was then that someone said 'Where the hell's Jeff?' No one had seen him for nearly two days.

'He's got my shirt.'

'And mine.'

'I gave him a pair of pants for cleaning.'

'There you are! The bugger's skinned out with the lot.'

'Collected all he could and beat it, eh? Should've known better than trust a bum like that.'

'Clever, the way he got us needing him and then ... '

I listened to all this and lots more like it, but said nothing. What was there to say? Yet I knew, I absolutely knew, that Jeff wasn't a thief. Strange in many ways, maybe, but not a crook. And there was still time ... he could still turn up before we sailed.

At noon we let go our moorings and anchored a little way off the jetty. The captain went ashore with the ship's papers, and by the time he got back in the evening, we were secured for sea. It was just a question now of waiting for the land breeze ... and Jeff. I still found it difficult to believe that he'd done us down. Next morning, though, the hands were called at dawn, and half an hour later the anchor was a-weigh and we were making sail out of the bay.

I was downcast. Those long, almost emotional, and yes, inspiring, talks we'd had about Australia and life in the outback – the hard, healthy life of the Australian bush. A life, I thought, that I might come back to one day. The arid wilderness of the Nullarbor Plain, with its black fellows moving secretly between the water holes ... and gold ... yes, gold ... one couldn't escape the lure of it.

We'd even started making plans, though looking back now, I guess that Jeff must have smiled inside him at some of them. When I paid off from *Olivebank*, I was to get myself back to Aussie somehow and serve the rest of my time on the coast there. Then we'd go prospecting. And when we'd made enough, and I'd got my tickets, we'd start up with a small ketch or something. Quite a few Finns and Swedes had done much the same.

But now ... Oh, well ...

March 4th

Olivebank stands east across the Spencer Gulf, then turns with ponderous grace and starts back west again. For two whole days she's been heading this way and that against a constant southerly wind and getting nowhere. Hemmed in by the York and Eyre peninsulas, and the curving line of islets between them, she is powerless to escape.

Why doesn't the Old Man anchor and wait for a slant, we wonder. But he never even considers the idea. We have left Port Lincoln. We are at sea. Harbours no longer exists for us, especially Port Lincoln, which for the past two mornings at dawn has appeared, first to starboard, then to port. And now again, an hour before sunrise, the lights of the little township can be seen twinkling, fine on the starboard bow.

To port, Thistle Island and the land beyond look very close – a continuous undulating band of black between the stars and their reflections. If a breeze springs up again we'll have to tack.

But meanwhile it's calm, quite calm and clear, and very still. At the distant high-pitched barking of a dog, the hills recede. In a moment they look a good two miles away. Only for a moment, though. As soon as the barking ceases, the land comes creeping back across a glassy sea – close up beside the ship, snuggling against her almost. And the stars crowd round, above and below, enclosing her.

March 5th

Koskinen, leaning his elbows on the pin rail in the starboard waist, sighs deeply. Occasionally he bends his head to sip at the mug of coffee held between his two great fists. But his eyes never leave the cluster of red-roofed houses on which the sun, starting up out of the sea behind us, has cast a flood of orange light, making the little township leap into sudden prominence out of the surrounding bush.

Koskinen sighs again. 'Liz blaady goot' he murmurs yearningly, 'jig-a-jig like angel.' At heart he is a simple fellow and means what he says. His conception of Heaven might well include rows of compliant angels laid out for his perpetual enjoyment. To be drunk, to love, to eat enormously and then relieve himself; through any of these he can attain to earthly Paradise, so why not in heaven too?

For the third time he sighs. Then tossing the dregs of his coffee into the sea, he wanders forward. Next moment his hearty grunts and groanings from the starboard 'heads' proclaim that he is once more in heaven or near it.

The second mate paces up and down the poop. He looks quite satisfied with things, but his eyes avoid Port Lincoln, as though he has decided that it can't be there.

Yesterday afternoon the Old Man vanished from the poop. We haven't seen him since. But now, while we are still finishing breakfast, he suddenly appears, gives the land one short, penetrating look and immediately sings out 'Ready about!'

'Ready about!' repeats the second mate in a startled voice. The rest of us take it up automatically, as we tumble out on deck – somewhat puzzled, though; because as far as we can see the Gulf is mirror calm in every direction.

After a hasty word with the Old Man, the second mate blows three blasts on his whistle as he comes thumping down the poop ladder. 'Wear ship! Fore and main clew garnets!'

By the time we are ready to haul, the situation has altered visibly. Now we can all see the dust cloud which the Old Man had spotted, forming on the crests of the hills behind Port Lincoln. Soon a few isolated catspaws come seeking out to us from the land, and the ship is beginning to cast slowly to starboard.

As yet, however, there is no more than a breath of westerly wind – barely enough to wear ship. Just enough, though; *Olivebank*'s head begins to pay off slowly, swinging in a wide sweep through north-west, north and on round. But still no way on her, till at last, stealing out across the water, from about north-west, comes a silver line of ripple – wind ripple.

The helmsman sees it first, and passes the word to the Old Man, who turns to give it a momentary inspection, then: 'Vast hauling!' and we wait at the braces, our eyes glued on the spreading ripple astern.

'Steer south east!' The helmsman spins the wheel amidships, then comes down off his grating to lift the cowl off the binnacle. A few moments later the breeze has almost reached us. High above our heads the royals flap lazily once, then fill. Shot through with sunlight, and barred by the shadows of their buntlines, the lower sails follow, bellying out between the yards.

'Haul square!' There's quite a ring in the Old Man's voice. We lie back with a will on sheets and braces. The smoke from the galley funnel wavers, then lies flat, streaming forward. The steward, a bumptious youngster, comes out on deck. He sweeps the scene with a haughty stare and nods his condescending approval, then disappears again.

The ship gathers way. The rising hiss of her bow wave breaks into a thousand gabbling voices as the wind ripple reaches her and passes on. Aloft a parral jumps; ropes creak as they tauten; a main lower topsail chain sheet slips a link with a loud clang, then quiet. *Olivebank* sighs deeply and lies over to port, stooping to the burden of a freshening westerly breeze.

And now men's voices are suddenly raised, from a lackadaisical murmur to cheerful shouts and laughter. Jokes are cracked. The watch below goes barging forward, chatting and chaffing and playing the fool, to disappear in a wrangling body into the forecastle. But not to sleep; soon the squawk and chirrup of a mouth organ, supported by forks drumming on the forecastle table, comes out to join the argument of wind and water. The houses of Port Lincoln float awhile with desperate persistence on a streak of mirage, then run together suddenly, like melting wax, and disappear.

By noon we have Kangaroo Island abeam, and *Olivebank* is already lifting and rolling to the first of the swell – that long unceasing movement of the ocean, running eastwards round the world in high south latitudes from one year's end to another.

The men in the forecastle feel her move. Squares of sunlight from the skylight overhead start to trace rhythmic patterns over and round the table. Cups rattle. A pile of seaboots and clothing in one corner topples over and has to be re-stowed. The singing and the shouting fade as men fall silent, listening to the wind. Fair wind!

This coming to life of the ship after weeks in harbour is disturbing. Like rising sap it makes men restless. No one in the watch below can sleep. One by one they stagger out on deck, blinking and clasping their scanty rags about pale and oddly female-looking limbs. Homeward bound! We feel it now at last, the ship and we. A wave of scarcely justified enthusiasm (there's a long tough haul ahead) runs through the little group collecting by the fore hatch and along the rail nearby. Absurd calculations are made, based on our present speed – about eight knots. Furious arguments spring up, and as quickly split into a dozen totally different and irrelevant disputes.

Leimbach comes forward with his concertina and sits down on the hatch. Eklund brings out his violin, his cousin Gustafsson a mandolin. Scheibel joins the group, but stands aloof.

One of the jungmän keeps bursting in with questions about the route to Cape Horn. The crowd get impatient with him; they are absorbed with their personal arguments.

'No, but how long must we be at sea?'

'Till the Trades some months ... In the Doldrums also months ... stop worrying.'

'But how long?'

'So long that you are playing your organ with two hands before Falmouth.' Koskinen is a coarse fellow, but he likes young Fågelklo, and gives him a friendly kick in the pants.

The other Replot boys bridle at once, but no one really cares ... To see the land slipping past and disappearing astern; to feel the lift and run of the ship and the first exciting breath of cooler winds – these are enough for the present. Leimbach sitting on the corner of the hatch is tearing off Tyrolean Waltzes. He crouches over his concertina smiling quizzically, as though in possession of some deeper secret of life than the rest of us.

As the ship clears the land and turns southwards, marching away into open ocean, the wind backs southwesterly and freshens. *Olivebank* lies well over, as though with her ear to the sea, listening for the tramp of approaching gales. One hatch board from every hatch is off, and the hatch cover flapped back to ventilate the hold. When you lean over and peer into the sounding darkness, you hear the brawl of water passing down her sides – bubbling up ahead of her as she dips, then rushing aft with the clamour of a fleeing crowd. The seas ring and thunder against her plating; unsecured cable clunks and rumbles in the chain locker forward. Down there is a whirlpool of urgent sound, drowning the music on deck.

Drowning the arguments too, until Scheibel's sharp voice breaks in with: 'If necessary there will be war'. Leimbach stops playing and looks up. Eklund and Gustafson play on softly to themselves.

'War? Fighting?' Koskinen looks sternly at the young German, who has trespassed on his own beloved territory.

'War is the heritage of the ruling races,' pronounces Scheibel.

'At sea we are safe,' observes someone mildly, 'None knowing where the wind is blowing us.'

'There is foreigners aboard.'

This is howled down at once. But the seed of uneasiness has been sown. Suppose there were someone on board with a radio transmitter hidden in the hold? And a U-boat waiting off the Horn?

One of the Ordinary Seamen, sitting on the main hatch, glances over his shoulder at the dark opening where a hatch board has been removed. 'You can't be sure with foreigners,' he mutters.

'Forget it,' The Donkeyman, grinning, drags him to his feet and pulls his cap over his eyes. 'They is all our boys.' He looks from one to the other, determined to stop the rot ... 'And soon we are disappearing in the sea. Do you ask for more?'

'What's the bleedin' time?' We all swing round. If Father Neptune had popped over the rail and said 'Tickets please', we couldn't have been more astonished than at the hoarse cockney voice and the sight of Jeff's tousled head, gaunt features and scraggy neck poking up out of the gap in the hatch cover behind us.

26.

West Wind Drift

We were flabbergasted. We didn't know what to do. Jeff clambered out on deck, and somehow managed this one-handed, while gripped under the other arm was a bundle of brown paper parcels. Each contained someone's laundry, which Jeff proceeded to hand out – except for one, which he put back under his arm. Then away forward to the forecastle, where we cleared his old bunk of the spare gear and rubbish which had collected there, and gave him a mug of coffee. After that Jeff was ready to face the Captain.

But the skipper thought otherwise. We gathered along the port rail in the lee of the galley to watch as Jeff shuffled aft down the starboard side in his usual crab-like fashion clutching his last brown paper parcel. It always surprised one how easily and swiftly he could move – turned a bit sideways, with one shoulder down. The skipper and the third mate were taking a turn on the weather side of the poop. Jeff stopped by the mizzen fife-rail and looked up at them. The skipper looked straight through him, and turned aft without a pause, to continue his pacing.

Next time he came back to the rail, it was exactly the same. Jeff was nonplussed. He offered his parcel to the third mate, who knew at once what it was. But the skipper had already turned to walk aft again, so he had to follow. Jeff shrugged and came back to where we were gathered.

'Left me standin' there like a bleedin' petrol pump in the Sahara Desert!' He sounded bewildered. 'Oo does 'e think 'e is anyway?'

'You will soon know dat' said the donkeyman. Then we all went forward.

A little later the third mate came to the forecastle door and called Jeff out on deck. 'You vill see de Old Man in de morning ... ven he is ready for you,' he said, and put out a hand for his parcel. 'You vill be in de port vatch ... de mate's' he added.

Jeff interested me more than ever now. I recalled how two days before we sailed he'd been unusually silent and bad tempered. He must have been in a bit of a quandary. The safe and comfortable little home he'd built up for himself, with well-watched points and carefully worked oracles, was about to disappear. In forty-eight hours he'd be alone and on the bum again. And for once he, of all people, hadn't made a plan. He was worried.

He reacted by taking it out on all of us, and of course we let him, because we were sorry for him. He swore at us for idiots, living insecure and uncomfortable lives, on a nasty rough sea for very little pay. Jeff was against the sea on principle. What's more, at this time of year, with autumn coming on, there'd be ice about in the Southern Ocean, he'd heard, and maybe gales all the way to the Falklands. And that wasn't all. What about the news from Europe? Talk of civil war in France, eh? And Germany ready to take advantage of it, what about that?

So what was it that had made Jeff change his mind? Or had he intended all along to come with us, and was everything else an elaborate smoke screen?

Next morning, with the wind off the land again and falling, Jeff was sent for as expected. I went along too, ostensibly to interpret if required; though this was hardly necessary, the skipper's English was excellent. But he let me stay.

The first thing he wanted to know was where and how Jeff had stowed away. So we all went down the main hold – the skipper, the mate and I, with Jeff leading. What we found there was a little miracle of ingenuity. By rolling back two bags at the fore end of the cargo, and bleeding a dozen more immediately beneath them, Jeff made a roughly rectangular cavity. Then short dunnage planks had been wedged in between the two uppermost bags on either side to make a platform, and the original two top bags rolled back on to them. This formed a sort of sentry box, open in front.

He'd also made a comfortable seat for himself with some of the empty bags he'd bled. Others served as blankets, and he'd even hung one or two across the front of his sentry box as curtains. Then he'd wedged other short planks here and there, to act as shelves and a table. And he'd provided himself with a small spirit stove; a kettle; mug, plate, knife, fork and spoon; a can of water and, of course, all the food he needed by 'working the oracle' with the cook and steward.

It was a gem of a set up, which could have kept him snug for weeks. He must have been sorry to leave it. But not knowing enough about ships to be sure he'd be safe – if the cargo shifted, for example – he'd come up as soon as he reckoned we were well enough on our way not to turn back and land him.

The Skipper examined the hide-out with interest and some amusement. But when he turned to Jeff, his face was stern. 'You couldn't have done all this on your own.'

'You'd be surprised, sir' said Jeff.

'Who helped you?' Jeff said nothing.

'How long were you down here?'

'A couple of days.'

'Who helped you?' Again there was silence.

The Skipper turned to me. 'He must have been helped,' he said 'Who was it?'

'Jeff's surprisingly strong, sir ... and I doubt if he'd trust anyone that much ... in fact I'm sure he wouldn't.'

Jeff made no comment and his face was expressionless. There was clearly nothing more to be said, so we climbed out of the hold again, the skipper first this time. 'Batten down fore and aft' he said to the mate, who followed him. Then he turned and went aft without another word.

The mate looked at Jeff. 'You'll work your passage. You know that?' he said. 'And I mean work ... You'll be in my watch.' Then to the third mate, in Swedish. 'The ship's a good bit by the head. I want at least a hundred bags brought aft from right forward, maybe more. Get him busy on it.'

So for the rest of the day Jeff, with one of the Ordinary Seamen in charge (I think it was Eklund), hove bags up out of the fore hold on a 'handy billy' tackle, ran them aft on a small porter's barrow we had on board, and stowed them in the after hold. He made no complaint, and again one was struck by the wiry strength and endurance of the fellow. But being in the starboard watch myself, it wasn't until next evening, during the 'make-and-mend' period between coffee and supper, that I got a chance to speak to him.

He was on stand-by, sitting on the main hatch, staring at nothing in particular, when I came up beside him.

'How're you doing?' It seemed a harmless opening. I had no idea what mood he'd be in.

'Makin' out' he said, so I plunged on.

'What about watching points, then? I thought you hated the sea .. and war scares in Europe ... and no pay ... and ... '

'They don't start till autumn ... after the harvest ... '

'What don't?'

'Wars don't.'

'Oh! ... Well anyway, how d'you think you'll benefit ... I thought you had it made in Aussie ... '

'I'd like to see grass again.' And that was all he'd say – then or later. He'd chat about this and that with me or anyone else. In fact he was his old confident and cheery self in no time at all. But if anyone got on to the subject of why he was there or where he was going when we got home, he'd clam up at once.

He was signed on the ship's articles as Jeffrey Spencer, but whose idea that was, his or the Captain's, I don't know. It certainly wasn't his real name.

We made a moderately fast passage to the Horn that year – thirty-six days – which wasn't as good as the year before, but above average for an early autumn run.

We kept rather a long way north. Most likely the skipper wanted to be sure of a landfall; because for more than a week before his dead reckoning told him that we had reached the longitude of the Diego Ramirez Islands, the sky had been too overcast for sights of the sun or stars. My diary for Easter Monday, April 2nd, records:

'The wind flew round into the south, and within an hour it was bitterly cold. Now at midday the watch comes on deck with stamping feet and swinging arms. The watch below crowd round the lee door of the galley with kits and teapot, then make a rush for the forecastle carrying their pile of hash, a loaf and tea. Both doors are shut and we sit luxuriating in the heavy warmth of our little home.

'That dear old smell of damp clothes, tea, Stockholm tar and tobacco, with a tinge of paraffin from the single oil lamp in the evening, will always bring back memories, happy as well as hard. It will recall the cold, calm nights when the ship lay under leaden skies, with the occasional gurgle of a passing sea along her deep sides; the tramp of the look-out up and down the forecastle head; great patches and lumps of brilliant phosphorescence floating past just beneath the surface – swishing, tumbling, bursting and passing by; the hoarse scream of a penguin, the low unearthly chuckle of albatross, and all around the soundless expanses of the Southern Ocean, waiting for a wind.'

Meanwhile, the ship was still 'by the head'. But it was no longer safe, with big seas boarding every now and then, to open hatches and bring more wheat bags aft. So she was a pig to steer, especially in heavy weather, when a high quartering sea would get under her counter, lay her over, then pour in over the quarterdeck bulwarks, filling the waist and dragging her round.

Surprisingly, though, Jeff was one of the few who really learned how to handle her. He'd been watching points, you see, and had quickly decided that in heavy weather the main deck, where we sometimes had to work up to our belts in a rushing torrent of water, and the upper topsail yard with a big sail hammering like sheet iron at the handful of men trying to tame it, were no places for a man of sense and sensibility.

He'd borrowed oilskins and warm clothing – mostly from the skipper, who secretly rather liked him, and the third mate, who had two of everything – and he didn't mind how long he stayed at the wheel or on look-out. He even did other people's tricks as well as his own for a few fags or extra sugar.

And Jeff was never seasick; that was another surprise, because we had quite a bit of weather over us on the way to the Horn.

But he wasn't going aloft for anyone nor to the braces in heavy weather. Throughout the voyage he worked the oracle with persistence and skill. He was never there when big seas were boarding. He could judge to the minute when hands were going to be called to shorten sail, and always managed to relieve the man at the wheel before this happened. It was wonderful to watch.

He was also ready whenever required to take over monotonous work which others found boring. He even earned himself a special corner in the galley (normally out of bounds to everyone) in return for keeping the fire banked at night and always seeing to it that there was plenty of the right sized coal in the bunker. The fact is that the man was good at his job – any job he chose to take on – and he chose carefully. That was how he became the best helmsman in the ship after Vihersalo.

27.

Fire Mountains

During the forenoon of the thirty-fifth day out from Port Lincoln, with a moderate north-westerly wind on the quarter, land was sighted dead ahead. Diego Ramirez, we thought; we'd been told to keep a bright look-out for high land the evening before. But we were wrong. By noon we had a mountainous coastline right across the bow and into the distance in both directions.

As we got closer, and the land rose higher out of the sea, we found we were approaching a great range of lofty snow-covered peaks, in other words the coastline of Tierra del Fuego – Land of Fire – somewhere between Cape Horn and the Magellan Straits. We turned away southwards, steering by the fall of the land. But when darkness came on, there was still an unbroken rampart of cliffs and mountains to port, as far as the eye could see.

In the middle watch, a half moon rose above the peaks, casting a mysterious sheen over snow fields and glaciers. The lower crags and gulleys fell into deeper shadow. As we passed the mouth of a deep gorge, two lights with an orange tinge – possible fires – appeared near the water's edge. They may have been from a small settlement, or fishermen out at night. One remembered tales of the Fuegan Indians, who built great fires of driftwood and hunted their old women through the mountains with dogs.

Just before dawn the small dark island which is the actual Cape Horn detached itself from the main coastline and was quickly swallowed again by further mountains as we approached. The wind came round to south west, so the main and mizzen courses were furled, in case the wind backed further and a sudden manoeuvre became necessary. But soon after sunrise we had cleared the last of the land and course could be altered to east-north-east by compass. Before evening, the snowy mountains of Staten Island were abeam to port.

That afternoon at coffee time, Jeff came into the forecastle with the customary bottle of Geneva, sent forward by the Captain to celebrate rounding the Horn. He seemed in great spirits.

'Nearly home, then? Another couple of weeks, eh?'

'What d'you mean, Jeff?'

'Only got to cross the Atlantic now, ain't we? Queen Mary does it in six days.'

We groaned. We thought we'd disposed of Jeff's 'narrow band of countries' theory when he first brought it up in Port Lincoln. Of course, he may have been putting it on, as part of some deep-laid oracle he proposed to work in the future.

'Afraid you'll be disappointed,' we told him. 'It's about thirteen thousand miles from here to Falmouth, and we'll have to go backwards and forwards and round about till we've covered them.' It was impossible to know what he thought of this because, as so often, he made no reply. But I could tell that he felt he'd made his point and was watching for the next opportunity to make another.

It may be worth trying at this stage to assess Jeff's position in the minds of the various factions on board. As I said earlier, the skipper and the mates liked him: he was willing, obliging and respectful at all times, and never made difficulties. The most he ever did when he disagreed with anyone in authority, or they said something to annoy him, was to fall silent.

The cook and steward were, of course, the principal targets for his study and attention. They could provide all sorts of small luxuries – not for himself so much, Jeff despised luxuries, but for others. In effect, therefore, the patronage of the catering staff was a marketable quantity, which allowed him to pass on favours of one kind or another to his friends and supporters. And, as I have also said, the crew in general liked him.

Nevertheless, there were a few who still wondered where he'd come from, why he'd joined us and what his true intentions could be. He'd been in Germany, hadn't he? And in Ireland? And his flat refusal to discuss the past or the future in any detail only added fuel to doubts in the minds of one or two. Vague suspicions aroused when he disappeared just before sailing, that he might have planted some infernal device on board, had been dispelled by his reappearance at sea. But what about a radio transmitter, on which an armed raider could home in to capture us?

On the whole, though, as the voyage progressed and they got to know each other better and better, they all tended to give Jeff the benefit of the doubt. So what was paradoxical about the situation was my discovery, after a while, that Jeff himself had more anxieties about the course of the voyage – and especially about the possible outbreak of war – than anyone else.

On a deep-sea voyage you may establish an almost terrifying intimacy with close companions; and being the only other Britisher aboard, I got to know the very innards of Jeff Spencer, or thought I had. He was a good talker, and actually quite fearless. It wasn't fear that kept him from going aloft, or down into the waist in heavy weather; it was pride. He'd have been downright ashamed to let himself be forced into doing such things. Antics like that were for fools like us.

But war, and the possibility of war ... 'It's a lot of nonsense ... ridiculous ... ' he insisted (Jeff hardly ever used strong language, by the way) ... 'My time in the army taught me that ... Waste of everything ... that's what; and after a long pause ... 'D'you think they could find a sailing ship out 'ere ... I mean a ship with no engine ... their hydrophones couldn't hear us, could they?'

So that was why he was with us ... why he'd chosen a sailing ship. One of the reasons anyway. And the other, of course, was because a sailing ship had to go where the wind blew her and couldn't turn back to land him once she was away at sea.

Soon after passing the Falkland Islands (we didn't actually see them this voyage) we ran out of the Westerlies into the calms and variable winds of the horse latitudes. I thought it might be interesting from now on to compare this trip, latitude by latitude as we moved up the Atlantic, with previous voyages. So I got out my diaries.

I chose the *Killoran* voyage, because the previous *Olivebank* passage home was full of little else but *Herzogin Cecilie*. I found that in latitude 28°31'S, we'd seen those strange little puffs of cloud in the sky which might have been bursts of anti-aircraft fire. So I kept my eyes open while on watch and asked Jeff to do the same in his watch.

And it happened again – one forenoon about two days later. 'That's what they are,' said Jeff, who'd been in the army for a year or so and probably knew. 'Ack-ack practice . firing from a ship over the horizon ... down wind, or we'd hear 'em.'

'If she was a destroyer or cruiser, she'd have to be about twenty miles away, or we'd see her,' I said. 'Those puffs are almost overhead. Would they be firing anti-aircraft shells that far?'

'Not likely,' Jeff thought.

'Unless it's a submarine. She'd be hull down and invisible at less than ten miles, I think.'

Jeff looked thoughtful. And just then Scheibel, who was in Jeff's watch came down the deck, paint pot in hand. 'What d'you think of that?' Jeff asked him, pointing to a small puff high up on the port side, that was dispersing rapidly.

Scheibel looked at it. Then put down his paint pot and looked harder. After a moment, he turned to Jeff. 'What?' he asked.

'Them puffs in the sky.' Another had appeared near the first. 'Is there any U-boats down 'ere?'

'What puffs?'

'Blimey! You can see 'em as well as me. Do U-boats have ack-ack guns?'

'I only see what it is my business to see' said Scheibel stiffly, and picked up his paint pot.

Jeff and I looked at each other. 'What's up with 'im?' said Jeff. 'Must be somethin' up.'

No more puffs materialised and after a while we stopped watching. But I could see that Jeff was bothered as he walked away – strangely bothered for Jeff.

A day or two later we picked up the South East Trades in about latitude 24°S, and soon left the overcast skies and cold, pale-green sub-Arctic water of the Westerlies for brilliant blue seas and sunshine in the tropics. As usual, all one's gear, one's soaked blankets and mattresses, one's seabag and everything in it was dragged out and spread over the hatches. The ship was soon festooned with strange possessions scattered around or hung up in the rigging to dry.

Jeff hadn't many possessions other than the warm clothing and blankets he'd scrounged from the skipper and third mate. But he had a few – a second pair of gym shoes, a towel, a teapot, some blotting paper, his kettle and spirit stove and a miniature iron. The iron interested me. I hadn't seen it down in the hold when we went down to look at his hide out.

'Did Clara give you that?' I asked, picking it up. He snatched it away from me. 'Arr' he said.

'To use with your spirit stove?'

He nodded non-committally.

'Was there any Clara?' I asked next.

'D'you think I'm soft? Give half me money to a woman?

For what?' He was hanging up his shirt and spare gym shoes in the shrouds. When he came down off the pin rail he said, as a sort of throwaway line: 'Me and me mum used to dhobi and iron fifty shirts a week when I was a nipper.'

So that was what he'd used the plank table for, down in his hide-out – with his towel over it, to keep the shirt collars clean, no doubt. He only ironed the collars, I supposed; that little iron, heated on his spirit stove, couldn't have done much more.

In the meantime he had now made himself permanent washer-upper and forecastle sweeper. He preferred that to more regimented jobs under the eyes of the mates. Anyway he was a first class 'Peggy'. And that crab-like shuffle turned out to be a remarkably stable mode of progression when the ship was rolling. You'd see him sidling through the door, looking both ways as always, and carrying a mountain of dishes or pots for the midday meal, which most other people would have dropped before they'd gone a yard.

And strangest of all – though I'd never have risked suggesting it to him – the bloke was happy. I remember one night on look-out, somewhere off Rio, I think – strong warm wind, sails billowing, stars like acid drops in a black sky – and suddenly there was Jeff beside me – open shirt, brown gym shoes, wary look and all. We stood for a while listening to the hiss and thunder of the sea under the forefoot. Then he said: 'You know, there's something in this. I wouldn't have thought it, but there is.' And I heard him whistling as he shuffled aft again.

28.

Doldrum Distractions

First blazing heat, then downpour; twirling the yards this way and that to catch every random puff; then calm and blazing heat again. One week, two weeks, three ... and still you're no further, maybe you've gone back a bit. The big sperm whales love these waters, where the Benguela stream, full of plankton and squid, and the fish and birds who feed on them, turns west to join the South Equatorial Current. You see the whales spouting, their great plumes of steam and water bursting upwards against jet black curtains of rain-cloud. We caught a large shark which had two empty milk cans, a fish-ball can and the heads of five *doradoes* in its stomach.

And all the time a sitting target for torpedoes. The Finns don't pay any attention to Jeff's anxious looks: they are neutrals, and *feel neutral*, except where Russia is concerned. They rather like the Germans and believe in them. I also try to reason with Jeff. 'We saw the lights of a steamer last night. She wouldn't be all lit up like that if there was a war on. Now, would she?'

Jeff looks unconvinced. Without a radio of any kind on board, it was only too easy to lose control of one's imagination. And Jeff was nothing if not imaginative.

It was Lasse Gustafsson, the lad from Kuopio, who thought of a boxing competition to cheer things up and keep us all fit through the lazy days of the North-East Trades, which must be just over the horizon.

There was only one pair of gloves, Gustafsson's, so

Blomqvist, the sailmaker, got busy on a design of his own –
skiing gauntlets with canvas bags stuffed with ropeyarns
sewn to the backs of them. It was a good attempt and
stopped any lasting damage to bones and skulls, but the
canvas was hard and abrasive compared with leather, and
one of the gloves had a seam right across it which scraped
people's faces. However, it was quite easy to rope off a
good sized ring between the main hatch and the bulwarks,
and everyone was keen – especially Gustafsson who, being a
champion welter-weight at home, offered to instruct the
others.

The jungmän from Replot had some lively bouts among
themselves. Gustafsson and his cousin Eklund had an interesting fight. But Horst Scheibel decided at once that he and
Leimbach would only fight each other. 'A German officer
must never risk humiliation at the hands of a foreigner.' So
he whaled into poor old Leimbach who, though every bit as
strong and rather bigger than Scheibel, was slow and
essentially good-natured. Scheibel made mincemeat of him
again and again. They even went on for several days after
the rest had packed it in. You saw them by the fore hatch
most evenings – having 'Strength through Joy' for Scheibel,
while poor Leimbach had to content himself with slowly
becoming 'refined by pain'.

But the most interesting situation arose when the sailmaker himself thought he'd like to have a go. He was a
great bull of a man – by far the largest in the ship – and
immensely strong. Yet his most interesting and worrying
quality was that he had absolutely no science, no training;
and his wild swings had such power and weight in them that
if they ever landed, they might well dislocate a shoulder or
break an arm – or a neck for that matter.

He was, of course, a kindly and cheerful fellow, like his
brother, the second mate. He certainly wouldn't have wanted
to hurt anybody. But equally certainly, he had no idea of the
damage his blows could do. Lasse Gustafsson tried to stand

up to him; but his scientific parries and feints simply didn't work against the Blomqvist sledge hammer. He was forced to withdraw. And then ...

'Let me 'ave a go ... '

Everyone turned to stare at Jeff, shuffling over to where Gustafsson had laid down his gloves ... 'Used to do a bit of this in the army,' he said, as he pulled them on ... 'C'mon Sails.'

The next ten minutes were an education to us all, not least to the sailmaker, who at first stood there rubbing the side of his jaw with his glove, clearly uncertain what to do or what was expected of him. They just weren't a pair in any sense of the word – the mighty Blomqvist, six foot three and a mountain of muscle: little Jeff, probably about five foot seven, but crouching and weaving and all hunched together; his chin on his chest; his left shoulder shielding, almost covering his face.

All at once Blomqvist lashed out with a mighty swing. It caught Jeff's shoulder and literally rolled over it. Then back again, missing Jeff's head by several inches as he ducked. Jeff edged forward sideways, crab-like. Blomqvist hammered one straight down on top of him, which ought to have squashed him flat. But he wasn't there; somehow he'd slithered a bit – just a bit – to one side. Then he darted in and landed a quick hook into Blomqvist's solar plexus, which made him grunt. Then out again in a flash – that is, it didn't look like a flash, more a sort of scurry, but it was far too quick for Blomqvist.

And so it went on. *Jeff:* in, out – in, out. *Blomqvist:* swing – whizz – no contact. *Jeff:* round the other way – in, out – in, out. *Blomqvist:* swish back-hand – hammer down. *Jeff:* duck – jump aside – down almost to the deck – dart in – step back. *Blomqvist:* roaring, falls over himself – thump on Jeff's shoulder. *Jeff:* change stance – lead with right shoulder – bobbing – weaving – darting. It really was a remarkable performance. I had boxed at school ever since prep-school days, but I'd never seen anything like this. What's more, I'd never seen anything taught like it. Nor had Gustafsson.

In the end it was the sailmaker who had to give up, out of sheer exhaustion. He flung his gloves down with a roar of laughter, and everyone laughed with him. Except Jeff, who smiled faintly, and sat down on the main hatch hardly puffed at all.

When I found him on stand-by later, he said ... 'You got ter use yer loaf at that game ... no good slashin' and tearin' about ... you got ter watch, see? And keep well down ... and gripped together. You can come up at 'em from under that way ... and you're difficult to 'it, see? Not so far to fall, neither.' It turned out, too, that for several years – in the army and afterwards in Australia – Jeff had made part of his living as a regular sparring partner. So there was yet another side to this extraordinary man.

The Trades, when they came, were disappointing. But after a few days of fairly steady north-easterly weather with clear skies, we began to see Sargasso weed round the ship and felt we were entering home waters. We also began to meet steamers, and spoke to one or two by flag signal.

Yet, Jeff still seemed ill at ease, and there appeared to be no way of reasoning with him. Throughout his life he had found that it seldom paid to depend on others or their advice. And I suppose that, being himself first and foremost a looker-after of number one, he expected (and preferred) others to be the same.

Then, somewhere south-west of the Azores and about the latitude of Florida, a British ship steamed past without answering our signal or our dipped ensign. I was afraid this would start Jeff off again, and I was right. That evening, being on day work, I settled myself in the fore crosstrees for a quiet read and a think, away from the noise and bustle of the forecastle. The wind was light and warm enough to keep me there well after dark. I thought I'd wait to see the moon rise and was surprised, after a while, to find that I wasn't going to be alone. Someone was climbing the weather shrouds.

To my astonishment it was Jeff – straight up to the foretop, over onto the topmast shrouds and on, as though he'd been doing it all his life. He swung himself across onto the upper-topsail yard and made himself comfortable with his back to the mast.

'I thought you never came aloft,' I said.

'Got to watch points a bit.'

'How d'you mean?'

'Didn't like that fella not answering us 's mornin'.'

'And so?'

'Well ... ' He was obviously not in one of his reserved or secretive moods. He'd come up here to tell me something, or maybe even to ask me; and I noticed now that he had his seabag with him, slung on his back. There wasn't much in it, of course, but still, it was an awkward piece of gear to carry aloft. 'Well, the way I sees it ... if we *was* to cop it, you'd 'ave a better chance up 'ere', clear of all the riggin comin' down on you, ... So you'd 'ave a chance of floatin' off and grabbin' onto somethin''. That was a long speech for Jeff, and I didn't know which bit of it to answer first. 'And another thing ... you'd be clear of the bloody explosion,' he added.

I sighed to myself. 'There isn't going to be any explosion ... ships often forget to dip their ensigns ... or the stand-by's sneaked below for something ... or they just can't be bothered.'

But he wasn't convinced. 'You got to watch it,' he said stubbornly.

We were silent then for a bit. I was casting round in my mind for some way of changing the subject. It was one of those nights when the sea seems to be full of phosphorescence. At times you're sailing through great swathes and patches of it, and everything that moves seems to gather it – fish if there are any, Sargasso weed, and deeper down great lumps of luminescence which might be anything. I pointed out some of these as they passed.

'Arr ...Phosphorous,' said Jeff ... 'I was in a watch factory once, where they used it ... '

'What was your job?'

'Night watchman.'

'Is there anything you haven't been?'

'Arr ... I ain't been a ballet dancer,' he said. And after a pause, 'but I wouldn't mind 'avin' a go ... You got to keep movin'.'

Jeff with his anxious look and crab-like movements was difficult to imagine as Siegfried or Romeo. But you never knew. You never knew with Jeff. And just as I thought this, there he suddenly was – standing on the crosstrees beside me. He'd leaped up, lithe as a cat, gripped a to'gallant shroud, and was gesticulating wildly to leeward with his other hand ... 'Look!' he half screamed 'torpedoes!'

And there, sure enough, were parallel tracks of phosphorescence, streaking towards us. 'Look out!' yelled Jeff, clinging to both shrouds. 'Hold on.'

And a moment later, the two tracks had swung away forward, crisscrossing ahead of us with the characteristic 'Poof! Poof!' and splash of dolphins and porpoises who've found a new playmate with a rushing, tumbling bow wave.

'What you make up 'dere?' The third mate's bull voice hailed us from down on deck.

'Dolphins' I called back. There was nothing else to say. He went aft again – shaking his head, I don't doubt. It was too dark to see.

'Time we went down,' I said to Jeff. He followed me without a word. And he never brought the matter up again, as *Olivebank* stood steadily northward through the trades, the horse-latitude calms, and then curved eastwards into the greyer windier regions of the North Atlantic westerlies.

We reached Falmouth 115 days out from Port Lincoln, but didn't anchor; the pilot launch came alongside in the offing with orders to discharge in Sunderland, so we bore away again up channel, close-hauled to a southerly breeze.

29.

A Hard Beat Home

The situation in Europe at this time – June 1934 – was, in fact, disturbing. Newspapers had come off with the pilot launch, including one or two weeklies from earlier on. Hitler was undoubtedly getting restive; and only a week or two before, the Disarmament Conference, on which great hopes had been set, ended in failure.

Lasse and I had decided that as soon as we'd served three years of our time for second mate, we'd take a spell and go skiing in Austria. Lasse had never tried mountain skiing. So when we reached Sunderland, I telephoned home to say that I was staying with the ship till she paid off in Mariehamn, and would then, I hoped, find another in the Baltic timber trade, to bring me back to London with my three years completed.

Before we left, Jeff managed to work his final (and to me most conspicuously successful) oracle of the voyage. He somehow succeeded in persuading the normally hard-nosed immigration authorities that he was a poor hard-done-by soldier lad, home at last after unbelievable sufferings bravely borne, which were no fault of his own. I didn't hear whether they actually wept.

However, when Captain Lindvall tried to invoke the law over Jeff (what law and what he hoped to gain, I don't know), the Immigration boys stood out firmly against him. One of them, in fact, said to me 'Can't let these foreigners do what they like with one of our own boys, can we?' Which I thought was grossly unfair to a skipper who'd befriended Jeff from the first and, as I said, rather liked him. We let it go, though, and Jeff went off with a note to my father, who said that he'd 'see if he could fit him in somewhere'.

I only saw Jeff once again – two or three years later – and, believe it or not, he was still with my father's firm, APV Co, where he'd made a lot of friends. Even so, I was surprised to see him still there. Had he changed, then? Or had he at last, perhaps, found a woman he could believe in and who believed in him? He was a remarkable man.

Twenty-one days out from Sunderland, we reached Marie-hamn. *Olivebank* paid off next day, and while at the office I heard that *Pestalozzi*, a thousand-ton barque, recently bought by Gustaf Erikson but too small for the Australian grain trade, was loading at Björneborg (now Pori) for London with a cargo of *split ved* (short planks for splitting into firewood).

She still needed more crew, and Lasse and I were both offered berths. We signed on at once. Nothing could have suited us better. Austria was already in a bit of a ferment. Chancellor Dollfuss had been murdered some two weeks ago; and about a month before that, Hitler had started tuning up the German Nazi Party by summarily executing several of its top people. Clearly we would have to make haste if we were going to have our skiing holiday in peace and relative comfort.

Two days later, I went aboard *Pestalozzi* at Pori, in south-west Finland, and after a week's leave in Helsinki, Lasse joined me. The cargo was coming aboard in armfuls, carried by great husky women who wouldn't stand any nonsense from anyone. We were told about the 3rd Mate of a Spanish steamer loading there, who had gone down the hold at dinner time and started chucking his weight about. He came up again an hour later with his hands lashed behind his back, no trousers and a tin can with a bolt dangling inside it tied to his John Thomas. Every time he took a step, the can bounced against his knees with an engaging cowbell effect. We kept our distance.

About half the hold was filled with cargo at Pori. Then we sailed up to Trångsund, the port for Viipuri, in an area at the head of the Gulf of Finland which has since become Russian territory. Here about the same amount of timber came aboard, to bring the cargo well up in the hatches. When these had been securely battened down, a deck cargo was built up six feet high all over, level with the tops of the galley and the two deck houses. Even so, *Pestalozzi* was still not deep loaded; but she looked like a London bus, and you had to climb down into cavities left free of cargo to get to the doors of the accommodation.

It was now early October. A plebscite in Germany about mid-August had confirmed Hitler as sole dictator and Führer, and nobody believed that anything much would come of the London Naval Disarmament Conference to be held in two weeks' time. On October 6th *Pestalozzi* sailed.

In all my four voyages in the Finnish square-riggers, I was shipmates with close on a 100 different men – 93 to be exact. A few in each ship were memorable. In *Pestalozzi*, the lad who springs most clearly to mind was young Bude (pronounced 'Bu'e'). He was an exceptionally cheerful youth with curly dark hair and red cheeks, who was friends with everyone and game for anything. Then a quieter, but equally cheerful and very gentlemanly young Dane called Sørenson. The second mate wore a cloth cap at all times and in all weathers, even when the rest of him was bundled up in oilskins and warm clothing. Then there was Kaunas, a beefy young Estonian with an ugly, humorous face. His real name was something far more complicated, so for some reason known only to the second mate, who thought of it, he was called after the capital of Lithuania – a practice which he evidently disliked, though he never complained.

And finally the Captain, whom this story is really about. I

shall call him K., though he must have died many years ago. To look at, he was small and wizened, and I don't remember ever seeing him in anything but a tweed overcoat buttoned right up to the throat, baggy trousers (though you couldn't see much of them), rough old rubber-soled shoes and an Astrakhan hat, like a sugar loaf only black, on top of his head. He must have shaved before we left, but never again throughout the voyage. He got shaggier and miserabler and more silent as the days, the weeks, then more than a month went by.

It took us three whole weeks to beat out of the Gulf of Finland and down the Baltic, against gale after gale, as far as The Sound. No one had expected this, and by the time we finally reached an anchorage off Copenhagen, our provisions were running low. We were confined to salt ströming and potatoes for every meal.

We kept sea watches while at anchor. Only the skipper went ashore in the agent's boat, but we wished him well and looked forward to his return with fresh provisions of many kinds. After more than two weeks on salt ströming and potatoes, anything and everything would have been welcome. The steward had a long list, to which we added with enthusiasm: fresh pork and lamb, butter, crates of eggs, various cheeses, maybe a few chickens which we could keep in a coop under the forecastle head; and the two Danish boys went further, with a whole list of delicacies which they knew their capital city could provide.

When the boat was seen coming off again, quite a few of the ship's company gathered round. A lifeboat davit was swung out and the fall overhauled to the water line. The first load it brought up was a case of whisky. The next was another case of whisky. Then the skipper came aboard. There was no third load.

We dispersed to our evening meal of ströming and boiled potatoes with a good deal of muttering and cursing. But Old K. had disappeared below, and before any plan of action could be agreed, three whistles from aft brought us all out on deck to find the wind freshening from South East and every ship in the anchorage (there were three besides ourselves) getting their anchors. It was the first fair wind for nearly a month. If it held, we'd be in London inside three days. We weighed and made sail with a will.

Throughout the night we went romping up the Kattegat at eleven or twelve knots. And soon after midnight the wind began to back. By daybreak, off the Skaw, it was blowing from due east and still freshening. It looked as though another two days at the outside would see us in London.

They very nearly did. We took our departure from the Naze of Norway, standing bold against the dawn behind us, and stood away south-west for the London River. We waved good-bye to Scandinavia and, we thought, to all our troubles, as the east wind continued to freshen. And just over forty-eight hours later, we raised the Galloper Light-Vessel at the mouth of the Thames.

Twenty-two days from Trångsund to Copenhagen, and another two and a half to the London River. Not bad. Not bad at all.

But within an hour of sighting the Galloper, the wind fell light. Then round it came into the south-west and began to freshen ... and freshen ... and freshen. There was nothing we could do but brace the yards sharp up and shorten sail while we waited for a shift of wind.

We waited seven days. And hour by hour the wind increased. It must have been one of the longest south-westerlies on record in those parts. It was certainly as hard a blow as any of us had ever encountered. We couldn't carry enough sail to manoeuvre the ship; she just lay there wallowing in the short, steep seas. First on one tack, then on the other, with her helm lashed and driving steadily to leeward.

Of course, for us lads it wasn't so bad. *Pestalozzi* wasn't deep-loaded, so she shipped very little water and we had a fine dry forecastle to live in. It was also well protected against spray by our deck cargo of firewood, which we plundered enthusiastically to keep our bogey stove roaring, day and night. In fact, the only jobs for the watch on deck were one hour on look-out, two hours feeding the forecastle bogey and one hour at the wheel. And this last, again, wasn't a very arduous duty, because the wheel was lashed; and by the second day of the gale, all except four small sails, had either been furled or blown to ribbons.

However, it was quite an experience. I remember one big sea crashing across the deck cargo and scooping up a whole pile of short planks, which it flung into the air, to be scattered by the wind into the sea to leeward. I also remember – without much pride – how we roared with laughter and yelled encouragement to the wind and sea.

'It'll cost the owners thousands,' we told each other gleefully. And quite mistakenly. Even the underwriters weren't going to be out of pocket. In those days, and maybe still, you couldn't insure timber deck cargoes from the Baltic in winter. No underwriter would accept the risk. So what the shippers did was to offer a handsome bonus to captains for every standard of deck cargo they succeeded in bringing safely to London.

So poor old Captain K., alone there on his poop, got very little pleasure out of the sight of his deck cargo being swept bodily away. He was sixty-eight, and this was his last voyage in a sailing ship. In fact, it was more than his last. He'd actually retired from the sea some years before, and had only been persuaded to come back for this one trip (to relieve a younger man who'd gone sick) by the offer of an extra-special bonus on deck cargo delivered safely.

He might well have succeeded in earning the whole of that bonus. Another two or three hours of easterly wind and we'd have been inside the Thames with all our cargo intact. But it just didn't go that way. And now, carrying the whole responsibility for the safety of his ship, her cargo and our own graceless lives, on his bent old shoulders, poor Captain K. stood there on his poop for six days and nights on end, with nothing but a helpless ship on a sea gone mad to look at; no music sweeter than the howl of a November hurricane, and after a while – no hope.

He seemed to shrink visibly, hour by hour, as though his whole insides were being sucked out of him by the force of the wind, till there was nothing left within that flapping husk of an old tweed overcoat, except two red-rimmed eyes under an old fur cap – first burning, then stony, and at last dimmed with an enormous pity. Not for himself, he was past that, but for the sea, condemned to an eternity of vileness.

And what finally broke him, on the seventh morning of the blow, was the sight, between two squall clouds, of the Naze of Norway, standing up bold and beautiful at dawn, about ten miles to leeward, exactly where we'd last seen it eight days before. It was then the poor old man sat down on his cabin skylight and cried.

I'd like to feel that we were sorry for him, and understood the magnitude of his personal calamity. But I doubt if we did – not then at any rate. We were young, and the whole thing had been a bit of a lark for all of us. Furthermore, the continuing diet of salt ströming and boiled potatoes (relieved only by a sort of plum duff for Sunday dinner) was hard to forgive.

We eventually reached London about mid-November, thirty-five days out from Finland. I was paid off there. And Lasse also wanted to leave the ship, of course. But this wasn't going to be easy. Immigration wouldn't let him land unless old K. agreed to pay him off, and K. refused.

That was when we committed a sin which we've ever since been unhappy about. We threatened that if Lasse wasn't paid off, we'd demand his release on the grounds that Captain K. would be certain to run his ship ashore before long, because he drank nearly a bottle of whisky a day. (He did, as a matter for fact, but no-one had ever seen him the worse for it.)

Anyway, it was a wicked thing to do, and there was no excuse for us. We were pitiless, with the stupendous pitilessness of youth. And although we would never really have split on the old man, we made no bones about threatening to. We were dead set on that skiing holiday.

We got it too. So neither of us made the trip back to Finland in *Pestalozzi*. Instead we collected our pay from old K. (though he still wouldn't sign Lasse off the ship's articles) and after a night at home, boarded a boat train at Victoria. Twenty-four hours later we drove by sleigh from the railhead to a small hotel at Obergurgl, in the Tyrol.

It was one of the finest skiing holidays that either of us had ever had. To be ashore for a spell was a luxury in itself; but to be skimming over snow-fields like swallows, and rolling about in snow – real snow, and warm sunshine with it – was a joy. Even when Lasse dislocated his shoulder, we only paused while the local G.P. yanked it back into place and strapped the arm to his side. Then off we went again – like swallows, was it? Or antelopes? We felt a bit put upon, when the doctor had the nerve to send us a bill for £3. It seemed a fantastic fee in those days for such a simple task. Anyway we paid it. And then it was time to get back to London. Or so we thought.

The Immigration boys thought otherwise. And, oh, were they charming about it! Looking back on it now, I realise that they were having a most enjoyable evening instead of a boring one, just because Lasse hadn't been signed off *Pestalozzi*'s articles, nor got his passport stamped on entering Britain.

They smiled. They were sympathetic. They were desolated. But oh, what a pity that they couldn't do anything about it. You see, he might have jumped ship, mightn't he? Not, of course, that they'd dream of thinking that Lasse could do anything so base! So illegal!

And we soon realised that they knew exactly what we had done. I expect K. had reported it. So, in the end, back Lasse had to go to Paris, where luckily there were friends he could stay with. And that was the last I saw of him or of sailing ships for nearly two years.

It was a sad parting. But we made the most of it while waiting for Lasse's transport, by going over our plans for a voyage round the world one day *in our own ship*!

But what of old K? We'd more or less forgotten about him by then. And it wasn't till over a year later – by which time I was serving as 3rd Mate in a British tramp – that I ran into another old shipmate, who'd been in *Pestalozzi* with us, I think it was Sørensen.

Naturally I asked what sort of passage home they'd had. 'Pretty good,' he said, ' ... as far as it went.'

'How d'you mean?'

'We went aground off the coast of Jutland.'

'Good God!' ... And then, 'Poor old K.'

My friend agreed. But rather grudgingly. He described the stranding and their efforts to refloat *Pestalozzi*, which ultimately succeeded. Fortunately the sea was calm. In fact, *Pestalozzi* had more or less drifted ashore.

Still, I felt rotten. To think that we, for our own selfish ends, had half predicted such a catastrophe. Not that we'd ever have expected it to happen, or even believed it possible, but we'd thought of it – even suggested it – and the sea had heard us.

Now, I'm not, in fact, superstitious. A ship becalmed – an unlucky eddy of current – misty weather and a low flat coastline – these are circumstances which have brought disaster to ships before and no doubt will again. It's the luck of the game – downright rotten luck – which can bring ruin to the smartest vessels and their captains. But even so, I wish we'd never said what we said that day in London. You can't be too careful what you say at sea.